THE CAT BEHAVIOR
answer book

The CAT BEHAVIOR

answer book

Understanding How Cats Think, Why They Do What They Do, and How to Strengthen Our Relationships with Them

2nd Edition COMPLETELY REVISED & UPDATED

ARDEN MOORE

Storey Publishing

The mission of Storey Publishing is to serve our customers by publishing practical information that encourages personal independence in harmony with the environment.

Edited by Deborah Burns and Lisa H. Hiley
Art direction and book design by Erin Dawson
Text production by Liseann Karandisecky
Indexed by Andrea Chesman

Cover photography by © annaav/stock.adobe.com, front, t.c.; Courtesy of Atali Samuel Photography, front, b.l.; © BilevichOlga/stock.adobe.com, front, t.l.; © carebott/Getty Images, back; © Kate Lacey, front, b.c. & b.r.; © smrm1977/stock.adobe.com, front, t.r.
Graphics/illustration by © Alexander Pokusay/stock.adobe.com, 36; © Natalyon via Creative Market, 13 background (and throughout)
Interior photography credits appear on page 218

Storey books are available at special discounts when purchased in bulk for premiums and sales promotions as well as for fund-raising or educational use. Special editions or book excerpts can also be created to specification. For details, please call 800-827-8673, or send an email to sales@storey.com.

Storey Publishing
210 MASS MoCA Way
North Adams, MA 01247
storey.com

Library of Congress Cataloging-in-Publication Data on file

Printed in the United States by Versa Press
10 9 8 7 6 5 4 3 2 1

I dedicate this book to all the cats in my life, past and present, who have made me a better person. Special paws up to Pet Safety Cat Casey, who assists me in my pet first aid and pet behavior classes and who loves visiting seniors and kids as a certified therapy cat.

Paws up to my pet-loving family, especially Julie, Deb, Karen, Kevin, Jill, Rick, Laura, Chris, Susie, Jim, and Geoff. And I thank Janice Dean, my high school journalism teacher, for her support and encouragement throughout my writing career.

CONTENTS

141

The Basics of Chowing and Grooming

Most cats lead a life of luxury, spending much of their day nibbling kibble, snoozing on the sofa, and taking care of their shiny coats. Find out why cats spend so much time grooming, learn how to tame tabby tubbiness, and brush up on the finer points of cat care.

177

The Ins and Outs of Life with Modern Cats

Indoors is safest, but even if your cat goes outside, there are many ways to enrich your indoor environment with tantalizing toys and stimulating setups. Learn about traveling with your feline companion and teaching an old cat (or a kitten) some new tricks.

PREFACE

Face the feline facts. Cats can be fussy, fascinating, frustrating, funny, and even a bit freaky. It's easy to be puzzled or perplexed as to why cats do what they do. Don't expect them to apologize or grovel—leave those actions to gotta-please dogs. Cats pride themselves on being candid about what they want and when they want it. I like to say that cats put the C in clever, the A in attitude, the T in tenacious, and the S in "so what." What are cats clearly not? Little dogs who purr.

Ever since I was a toddler, I've shared my life with cats. My feline friendship began with a cool Siamese named Corky, who joined me swimming in our backyard lake. These days, I team up with a confident, comedic ginger cat named Casey who assists me in pet first aid trainings and pet behavior classes all over the United States as well as in live, interactive Zoom classes that draw students from all over the world. Together, we are training a new member of the team, a crowd-pleasing red tabby named Rusty who lives for performing tricks.

For more than two decades, I have been a student and teacher of all things c-a-t, and I'm continually learning from the world's top cat experts. When people learn what I do, they are as curious as, well, cats, to find answers. In person, at conferences, and on radio/TV and livestream shows, I am asked: *Why does my cat … ? How can I get my cat to stop … ? What is the best way to teach my cat to … ?*

> **When people learn what I do, they are as curious, as, well, cats, to find answers.**

That's why I wrote *The Cat Behavior Answer Book*, originally published in 2007. A lot has happened in the cat world since then, though. A major feline revolution is under way that cannot be ignored—nor should it. More cats live in households than dogs. More people are willing to admit to being "cat daddies" or "cat moms." It's cool to love and live with cats.

Today's cat world includes cat cafés and new terms like *catio* and *catification*. Some of the most popular social influencers on Instagram and Facebook purr. There are new cat careers, including professional cat sitters, feline-only veterinary practices, cat detectives, and feline fashion designers.

You hold in your hands the completely updated guide to really getting to know and care for your twenty-first-century cats. Paw through these pages with an open mind and a willingness to be enlightened, educated, and a bit entertained. Your cat just may thank you . . . in his or her own feline way.

Paws up!

Arden Moore

Feeling Fine about
BEING FELINE

Ah, the life of a cat. It all seems so, well, purr-fect. Guaranteed meals. Plenty of time for napping. A personal assistant to tidy up your litter box. It is easy to feel a tinge of envy for our felines, but how much do we really know about our cats?

For starters, we may adore our furry friends, but the ancient Egyptians literally worshipped them. Centuries later, the tide had turned and the superstitious inhabitants of merry old England, believing black cats to be witches in disguise, burned thousands of them at the stake.

Loved and loathed—that's been the cat's fate through the centuries. Fortunately, feline popularity is on the upswing with more cats than dogs residing in American households. Many of us are drawn to their

beauty, their playfulness, and their feline mystique, not to mention the fact that they don't need to be walked twice a day and usually house-train themselves.

In this section, I introduce to you the many aspects of being a cat. For one thing, they like to ponder. After all, they waited an extra 10,000 years or so after dogs were domesticated to make sure hanging out with humans would be worth their while. They like to pounce, which explains how your ankle may be mistaken for a heavy-footed mouse in the hallway. They like to be pampered and will lure you with purring to obtain a cozy lap, a fishy treat, or a nice scratch under the chin.

Cunning, candid, and clever—cats have these characteristics and more. Read on!

A REAL SMARTY CAT

Our household contains an Australian shepherd, a miniature poodle, and a Bengal cat. The two dog breeds are known for their intelligence, but this cat, aptly named Mr. IQ, is no slouch when it comes to brainpower. He comes on cue, walks on a leash, rides in a pet stroller, and reads my hand signal to sit politely for a treat. How smart are cats, and how do they learn?

If there were a pet version of the popular game show *Jeopardy!,* your trio would trounce the competition, paws down. That furry bunch packs a lot of brainpower, and you may not be surprised to hear that cats learn similarly to dogs and people. They have complex brain structures and good long- and short-term memory. They rely on observation, imitation, and trial and error to try to solve problems. As creatures of habit, they often are able to use household routines to their advantage.

For example, many cats learn to open doors from watching humans manipulate the knobs. A friend of mine has a Norwegian Forest Cat who figured out how to paw open the door that leads into the garage. To keep her cat from sneaking into the garage (fortunately, Sheba has not figured out the garage door opener on the wall), my friend had to add a deadbolt lock to the inner door.

As you've proved with Mr. IQ, cats can be trained to do any number of behaviors, given the right motivation. Cats are big believers in the what's-in-it-for-me philosophy. Whereas most dogs tend to perform to please us as much as to reap the treats, cats are more likely to decide what they'll do and when they'll do it. If they can reasonably determine that you will come through with an acceptable reward, then they may participate in coming when called, sitting for a treat, or doing some other trick.

Finally, cats are smart enough to become masters at manipulating us. Whenever I head into the kitchen, one, two, or all three of my cats will follow me and perch on the kitchen island to see me at "eye level." Casey, the talker, will lead the persuasion act by vocalizing a sweet *mew* when I open the door to the laundry room where the coveted treat jar is stored. Mikey and Rusty then join in the bid for treats by looking at me with soft eyes and emitting soft *mews.* That's my cue to come out into the kitchen holding three kitty treats.

Of course, I know these guys are clever enough to recognize my weak spot and work it to their advantage, but I happily comply. Who's the truly intelligent being now? 🐾

Test Your Cat's IQ

Just how smart is your cat? One informal way to test your cat's intelligence is to evaluate his ability to discern *object permanence*. Although originally designed to look at stages of cognitive development in babies and toddlers, this test can be applied to cats and dogs.

Show your cat a coveted object in plain view, such as a favorite toy mouse or special treat. Then hide the mouse by placing a file folder or other solid object in front of it. To be ranked as "smart" as an 18-month-old child, your cat should know to look behind the object for the item, rather than thinking it has disappeared entirely once out of sight.

Supersmart cats, capable of thinking like a 2-year-old child, will also be able to follow the trajectory of an object that moves out of view. In other words, these cats should be able to predict where a live mouse that scoots out of sight under a sofa will reappear and use that knowledge to pounce as the mouse reappears.

Animal behavior experts report that most dogs figure out where the mouse will come out from under the sofa, but most cats do not. This may explain why some of us have more mice in our houses than we'd like.

PREDATOR AND PREY

I love watching my two young kittens bat around toy mice and chase the feathers on a wand toy. Why is the prey drive already so strong in such young animals?

While we usually think of cats as mighty hunters, they actually fill the role of both prey and predator, depending on the other species involved. Let's start with the predator role. Domesticated cats have retained much of the gene pool from their wild cat ancestors. Scientific studies reveal that lions, tigers, and other wild cats share 95 percent of DNA with house cats. Yes, there is a direct DNA link between the mighty lion in the jungle and the pair of tame tabbies purring peacefully on your lap.

All cats are genetically programmed to hunt. And all cats—wild and domesticated—prefer to be solitary hunters, with the exception of lions. In keeping with their size, our household cats focus on small mammals and birds. Interestingly, most biologists regard cats as small mammal experts and bird opportunists because cats tend not to be very good at catching birds unless the birds are sick, young, or ground nesting.

Predatory behavior is innate. Kittens early on show a tendency to crouch, stalk, chase, and pounce on their littermates, all kinds of toys, and human ankles. Just like us, they learn through trial and error, and their play sessions help them increase their speed, refine their leaping abilities, and hone their hunting skills.

Their moms also teach them by example. Outdoor cats often bring home a dead mouse or bird to their litter and eat it in front of the kittens to demonstrate the necessary behaviors. She will progress to presenting a dead animal to the kittens to eat themselves, and finally, will bring home a nearly dead creature for the kittens to finish off.

These experiences hone their hunting and killing skills. For indoor cats, the prey happens to be a store-bought toy or perhaps your fuzzy pink slipper. But the lessons learned are the same, and many kittens who learned nothing about hunting from their mothers quickly figure out how to catch and kill prey as adults or even earlier.

When the tables are turned and cats become the prey, they tap in to their survival skills. When faced with a real—or perceived—threat, felines react in one of three ways that all begin with the letter F. They freeze, flee, or fight. When a household cat confronts a noisy vacuum cleaner headed his way or finds himself outside facing an unleashed dog, his first response is usually to flee if at all possible, either by diving under the bed or by scooting up a tree. A cornered cat can fight fiercely, however, as many a startled (and scratched) dog has discovered. The very tools that make them effective predators become their best defense. That must be where the phrase *to fight tooth and claw* comes from. 🐾

feline fact

A group of kittens is called a kindle, but a group of adult cats is called a clowder.

THE ABCS OF C-A-T

Every day, my young tiger-striped cat, Felix, amazes me with his physical abilities. I can't believe how effortlessly he can jump from the kitchen floor to the counter to the top of our cabinets, where he calmly peers down at me. He never seems to miss when I toss a paper wad for him to catch with his front paws, and he appears to glide, not amble, when he walks. What are some physical traits cats have?

Although there are more than 45 distinct cat breeds, nearly 95 percent are what I refer to as "meowvelous mutts." Most domesticated cats range between 9 and 13 pounds with the smallest feline breed, the Singapura, topping out at 6 to 7 pounds and the largest breed, the Maine Coon, topping the scales at a hefty 20 to 25 pounds. Big or small, all of our feline friends share these five amazing physical traits.

Flexibility. Cats sport flexible spines, muscles, tendons, joints, and ligaments that allow them to run, jump, and land effortlessly. They can shrink or expand their spines easily, which explains how they can fit in tiny places to catnap and leap across wide-open spaces. In fact, they rely on more than 500 muscles to run, leap, and jump.

Paws with claws. Cats have cushioned pads on their feet and curved retractable claws that enable them to grip different types of surfaces and prey. They are known as digitigrades, which means they walk on their toes, much like ballerinas do during a performance. By comparison, people walk on the soles of their feet, making their walking style known as plantigrade.

Unusual walk. When cats walk, both legs on the same side move together in a gait called the pace. Camels and giraffes naturally exhibit this gait, as do some breeds of horses. This is different from a canine gait in which the legs move diagonally (right front and left hind, left front and right hind).

Cool coat. Their coats are designed to protect them from weather extremes (hot and cold) and to heighten their sense of touch.

Spiky tongue. The feline tongue sports a patch of barbs known as papillae that aid in grooming as well as serving to scrape meat from bones and to lap up water. Interestingly, there are no taste receptors located on this part of the tongue. 🐾

feline fact

Hairball is such a yucky word. The scientific name for that hacked-up mess is *trichobezoar.*

17

WHERE'D YOU GO, KITTY?

When I get ready to leave the house, I always call out to my cat, Clara, to make sure I know where she is. It gives me peace of mind. She usually doesn't respond, and I have to look all over for her. Often, I finally find her in a new hiding place. I know she can hear me. Why is she ignoring me?

It sounds like Clara has been taking some "hearing" tips from my cat Casey. Like you, I don't want to risk him darting out a door left ajar by a repairman or one of my guests. Clara is choosing to

ignore you because she is comfortably settled in a cozy spot. Don't take it personally. She is being, well, a cat. She doesn't see the need to please you like dogs do.

My advice is to pay attention to all of Clara's napping spots in your house. Search those spots first. Cats like to head to safe spots for their many mini naps of the day and prefer tucked-away places. Then check spots that might offer some new appeal, like a basket of clean laundry waiting to be put away, or an open drawer or cabinet door. (And always check those open drawers and doors before closing them, to avoid trapping a curious cat inside!)

If you still can't find her, tempt her appetite by shaking a jar of her favorite treats to flush her out of her hiding spot. I'm sure she'll hear *that*—it works every time with Casey! And I applaud you for getting into the habit of always knowing where your cat is inside your home before you open the front door and leave. 🐾

Now Ear This!

It may surprise you to learn that cats hear five times better than we do and even better than dogs. Credit their ability to rotate their cone-shaped ears independently like mini satellite dishes. With 32 muscles in each ear, a cat can quickly rotate them 180 degrees. This ear design allows felines to zero in on sounds coming from different directions and at varying distances and volume levels. With a mere six muscles per ear, I can barely wiggle my earlobes!

Cats use their ears to balance and land on their feet from a fall. Fluid in the ear canals tells the brain which way the cat's body is moving. They also use their ears to communicate their moods. They are not poker players—they don't bluff. A curious cat will point its ears to show interest. Sleepy, relaxed cats have ears to match, while scaredy-cats and hissed-off cats flatten their ears against their heads.

Ears can give clues to health, as well. If you see your cat vigorously shaking her head or scratching her ear, she may have ear mites, a bacterial infection, a food allergy, something in her ear, or waxy buildup in the ear canal. All of these situations warrant a veterinary visit. When applying ear medication at home, never use a cotton swab; you risk rupturing your cat's eardrum. Ouch! Instead, be calm and patient. Put the ear product on a cotton ball or gauze and gently massage the ear. Now that is some good "mews" worth listening to!

STARING EYE TO EYE

My black cat, Teddy, has large, round, beautiful green eyes. Sometimes I try to engage him in a staring contest, but you probably know the outcome. Teddy seems to always win. I rarely catch him blinking. How can he keep his eyes open for so long? And can he see better than I can?

Cats are more squinters than blinkers. The expression *in the blink of an eye* carries added meaning with cats, especially when they're in hunting mode. If a cat blinks—even for a fraction of a second—it could mean losing sight of prey. In the wild, that could mean the difference between a meal or going hungry. For domestic cats like Teddy, it's more likely to mean losing track of the treat you just tossed him that rolled under the refrigerator.

In your friendly stare downs with Teddy, you may notice that when he does blink, his upper and lower eyelids rarely meet. Cats also have an almost transparent third eyelid, called the nictitating membrane, that moves diagonally. Its job is to keep the eyes moist even when a cat is in an intense, nonblinking stare down. That's a big reason why Teddy wins the staring contests with you. (See also Eye Candy Time, page 63.)

Cats surpass us in seeing movement due to their superior peripheral vision. Their pupils can dilate wider to capture more of a panoramic view than we can. They can see faraway objects and are especially adept at detecting movement even at a distance. However, cats have poor up-close vision. This may help explain why a cat fails to see a piece of kibble or a treat right under his chin and has to rely on his sense of smell to detect it.

Cats can navigate in dim light, thanks to the colored portion of the eye call the iris. The iris muscles open and close to regulate the amount of light that enters the eye through the pupil. Cats can see about six times better in dim light than we can and that aids them during their prime hunting times—dusk and dawn. It's a popular misconception that cats can see in total darkness.

When exposed to bright light, their iris muscles shrink their pupils to the size of slits to allow them to see safely without damaging their eyes.

When it comes to detecting colors, however, we win. Recent studies confirm that cats do not see only in black and white. They can see shades of blue, green, and yellow, but cannot see reds very well.

Feline Eye Facts

Feline eyes come in three main shapes: almond, slanted, or round. Interestingly, a cat can sport one round eye and one slanted or almond-shaped eye and still have good vision.

All cats are born with blue eyes. In some breeds, such as the Siamese, the eyes remain blue, but with most cats, the color gradually changes to green, gold, or brown.

Smaller felines who hunt low to the ground have vertical pupils, but big cats such as lions and tigers have round pupils.

GLOW-IN-THE-DARK EYES

When I walk around my house at night in dimly lit rooms, sometimes I am a bit spooked when I see my cat. Precious is a sweet Siamese cat, but at night her eyes seem to glow red in the dark, giving off a devilish look. I notice this most after I've watched a scary movie on TV. What causes her eyes to glow red at night?

Timing is everything. You are more apt to be a little jumpy after watching a horror movie, but don't worry about Precious. She is not possessed by the devil. Her large pupils are designed to operate far better in low-light conditions and the dark than our eyes are. The best times for felines to stalk prey is when it is most active—at dawn and dusk. Although cats cannot see in total darkness, they do see better than we do even in the full moonlight.

Holding your cat in your lap, take a look at her eyes under a bright lamp. Notice that the pupils are elliptical in shape, compared to our circular ones. In the lamplight, the pupils become narrow slits to protect the sensitive retinas from damage. Now turn off the lamp and notice that her pupils dilate to accommodate the lower lighting. In very dim light, the pupils will fill her eyes, making them look almost completely black.

As for that red glow, it is caused by light reflected from a layer of tissue called the tapetum lucidum, which lines the back of the eyeball behind the retina. It acts like a mirror, reflecting light that was not absorbed the first time it passed through the retina back through the eyes onto the light sensor cells in the retina. The result is an eerie glow as your cat's eyes catch a beam of light in a dark room. 🐾

feline fact

Gold and green feline eyes reflect a green glow at night, but blue eyes glow red!

THE FELINE NOSE KNOWS

My cat, Freddie, loves food. And I swear he must be part bloodhound. He can be snoozing in the upstairs bedroom, but no matter how quiet I am, he'll come bounding down the stairs just as I am about to put a piece of cheese in my mouth. How in the world does he know when I am sneaking a snack?

With cats, the nose really knows what's going on. When it comes to this sense, cats easily best us. There are about 200 million odor-sensitive cells in the feline nose, compared to our paltry 5 million. Cats are just a sniff behind dogs, who can have up to 300 million such cells. If you dropped a piece of your cheddar cheese in a bathtub full of water, your cat could sniff it out. Now that's a powerful nose!

Cats learn about their environment by sniffing out information. They communicate with other cats by marking objects with their personal odor. Each time a cat rubs his head on an object (including you!), claws at the sofa, or uses the litter box, he is releasing scent signals for other cats to sniff, download, and interpret. Cats don't need to rely on Wi-Fi or high-speed cable to communicate. They let their noses do the talking! 🐾

WHY WHISKERS?

My young daughter recently took her kindergarten scissors and trimmed all the whiskers off our cat. Of course, I was very upset with her, because I know cats need their whiskers to find their way around, but I realize that I don't really know how they work. What happens when a cat loses his whiskers?

Most people realize that whiskers serve as measuring tools for most cats. The whiskers along the sides of the face size up small openings to alert them if their bodies can fit through without getting stuck. Chubby cats sport longer whiskers than skinny felines.

But whiskers serve other vital purposes. Cats use the long, protruding whiskers along their muzzles to rotate and scan for signs of prey or an object in the dark. What is amazing is that the whiskers don't have to actually touch an object for a cat to realize it is there.

Bundles of nerves in the whiskers supply information to the cat's brain, delivering almost supersensory abilities. I often equate the power of feline whiskers to the "Spidey sense" of superhero Spiderman.

Cats also have delicate whiskers above their eyes. Like our eyelashes, these whiskers activate a blinking reflex that automatically shields their eyes from flying objects or debris. Wispy whiskers under the chin sense objects from below. Whiskers on the front legs assist in safe landings and aid in sensing the presence of prey.

Whiskers can signal feline moods. Pay attention to your cat's whiskers when she goes on the alert or appears content. When relaxed, a cat's whiskers are held slightly to the side. But when a cat gets intrigued or feels threatened, the whiskers automatically tense up and point forward.

Without her whiskers, your cat's sense of balance, depth perception, and warning systems can be altered slightly. Veterinarians recommend keeping a whiskerless cat inside until the whiskers grow back, which can take two or three months. 🐾

Whiskery Facts

Whiskers are technically known as vibrissae. If your cat will tolerate it, grab a magnifying glass and take a close-up look.

A cat's whiskers are about twice as thick as the hair on their coat, and the roots of the whiskers are about three times deeper than hair roots.

Cats sport 8 to 12 long whiskers on each side of their upper lip. They lose a few whiskers at a time as part of the normal shedding process, never losing them all at once.

Some feline breeds are at a whisker disadvantage because they lack long whiskers. The Cornish Rex and the American Wirehair, for instance, sport short curly whiskers. The Devon Rex has a limited number of whiskers while the Sphynx has none.

PAIN? WHAT PAIN?

I often have to shoo Phoebe off my kitchen counters and the top of my bookcase. She loves to leap and perch on high places. But for the last couple of days, she's been sleeping more than usual and seemed content to hang out on the floor. Then I noticed that she was limping and her back leg was swollen. My veterinarian took X-rays and identified that Phoebe has a hairline leg fracture. She gave her pain medication and antibiotics. I can't imagine the pain Phoebe was going through. How could I miss that she was coping with a broken leg?

Cats in the wild and household cats instinctively hide any signs of pain or illness to prevent being an easy target for predators, real or perceived. They are masters at masking pain, even from people who love and protect them.

I remember as a child petting my cat, Corky, who was acting unusually quiet, especially for a normally talkative Siamese. My hand glided down his torso and I felt a warm, wet mess by his hind leg. He had somehow cut his leg severely. He never yowled or flinched. He needed stitches and recovered completely, but I can still remember how stoic he acted.

By comparison, dogs dig pack mentality and approval. They are far less shy to let their pet parents know that they have a cut paw, an upset stomach, or a pulled muscle. Some even crave attention to the point of overexaggerating

an injury to garner attention from their favorite people.

Bottom line: Don't dismiss signs that your cat is just not "acting right." Get into the habit of petting Phoebe with a purpose at least once a day. Glide your hand over her from head to tail. Look for cuts, fleabites, and lumps, and notice if she flinches when you touch her legs and tail. Take note of any changes in her eating or bathroom habits and report them to your veterinarian. Your vigilance can help keep Phoebe healthy for many, many years.

I also advocate having your veterinarian treat your cat to a full physical exam with blood and urine tests at least once a year. An annual exam may catch a medical condition in your cat when it can be treated in the early stages and possibly extend your cat's life. 🐾

Signs of Pain and Illness

Because cats prefer to hide any signs of weakness, we need to be attuned to subtle hints of injury or illness. Here are some clues to look for and report to your veterinarian.

- Not interested in eating
- Drinking much more water
- Urinating outside the litter box
- Sudden weight loss
- Bad breath
- Changes in sleep habits

- Changes in social interactions
- Changes in grooming habits
- Becoming more vocal
- Suddenly hiding and declining attention
- Showing less interest in playing or toys

SAVORING SLEEPY TIMES

Gracie, my gray-striped tabby, has quite the contented life. It seems that she sleeps all night and most of the day. I wish I could log half the amount of sleep she does. Why do cats seem to sleep so much, and how does their sleep differ from ours?

I understand why you might be a bit envious of Gracie. Cats have the coveted ability to fall asleep and wake up quickly. Their keen senses of smell and hearing alert them if a perceived danger is near. They are truly the Rip van Winkles of the world, averaging 17 to 18 hours of sleep each day, or about two-thirds of their entire lives. In fact, they sleep about twice as much as most other mammals.

Cats don't sleep for multiple hours at a stretch—rather, they are champions of

the power nap. Because cats are crepuscular, they are more active at dawn and dusk and do more sleeping during the day. How many hours they sleep each day is influenced by their age (fast-growing kittens tend to sleep more than adult cats), how safe they feel (sharing a home with a cat-pursuing dog would keep most cats wary and awake), and the weather (which explains why your cat may carve a tunnel under your bedspread to snooze in during a snowstorm).

Gracie is like other cats. She goes through a daily cycle: eat, sleep, potty, sleep, groom, sleep. You mention that Gracie seems content. Make sure that you are not confusing contentment with boredom. Bored cats sleep more than ones who interact and play with people and other pets in the home. Encourage a few play sessions every day. Even 5 or 10 minutes will activate her brain, work her muscles, and give her some cool memories to take with her when she dozes off into dreamland.

A cat suffering from insomnia is as rare as a field full of four-leaf clovers. Having trouble reaching dreamland is just not part of the feline scene. If your cat ever does experience sleep deprivation, I urge you to book an appointment with your veterinarian to have her examined. She may have a health problem that should be addressed.

Here are some favorite napping places for cats.

- Your lap

- Under a blanket

- Your bed and maybe even your pillow

- High perches like the top of a cat tree

- Snug spaces like cardboard boxes and open dresser drawers

- Warm places to catch the sun or near a heat vent 🐾

feline fact

Cats are champion sleepers, but bats and opossums log a few more z's. Those animals average 20 hours of sleep each day.

DIVING INTO DREAMLAND

I love watching my cat sleep. He moves a lot and even makes little squeaking sounds at times. His legs quiver and his whiskers move. Is he dreaming?

Cats do dream, but we can only speculate on the subject matter. It might be that your cat is reliving the brilliant capture of a wayward fly buzzing near a sunny window or a particularly speedy sprint down the hallway. Perhaps he is recalling with amusement how he charmed that final piece of broiled tuna off your dinner plate and into his own bowl.

We do have scientific evidence that cats dream. As with humans, feline sleep falls into two types—REM (rapid eye movement, which is when dreams happen), and non-REM (deep sleep). You will know your cat is in REM sleep because he is apt to twitch his legs, wiggle his whiskers, and subtly move his eyes behind his closed eyelids.

Studies using electroencephalograms (EEGs) to read brain activity in sleeping cats have indicated that cats are in the REM sleep stage for about 30 percent of their sleeping time and that their brain wave patterns during REM are similar to ours. In comparison, we spend about 20 percent of our sleep time in the REM stage (although human babies spend up to 80 percent in REM).

When cats are not dreaming, they are in the deep sleep phase. This is the time when the body goes to work repairing and regenerating bones and muscles and bolstering the immune system to fend off disease. The only movement you can detect during this sleep stage is the quiet rise and fall of the chest that indicates healthy breathing. 🐾

FACTS ON FELINE LOVE

My super-sweet kitty, Bubba, likes to cuddle with me and to follow me around the house. He is very friendly and affectionate, and of course I love him to pieces. This may be a silly question, but I've always wondered—are cats capable of loving us or are they just being nice because we give them food and shelter?

It's not a silly question but it doesn't have an easy answer. I would be able to give you a more definitive response if I could speak cat and ask the feline world directly. Cats are candid creatures, and I'm certain they would reply honestly.

Without that ability, however, defining feline love can be tricky. What we do know is that cats clearly express emotions. They get angry and they show fear. They display contentment and express excitement. As for interpreting cat love, cats definitely form attachments with people in their lives who make them feel safe and who shower them with attention.

Cats convey affection toward their people in numerous ways, including delivering soft-eyed winks by half-closing both eyes at once, twitching an upright tail, and delivering head bonks,

feline fact

Ancient Egyptians were major cat advocates. When a beloved cat died, family members would shave off their eyebrows in mourning.

a behavior also known as bunting. The next time you lock eyes with your cat, try giving him a few soft winks. I bet he returns the favor. And notice that when he sees you enter a room or hears your voice, his tail probably pops lazily up in the air with the tip twitching just a bit. See if he expresses affection by purposely bumping the top of his head against your forehead, hands, or shins.

When I moved a few years ago, I met Baxter, our neighborhood's community cat. He is a fluffy black-and-white cat who takes a long time to build trust with humans. I began taking over the evening meal-feeding duties, placing Baxter's food bowl on our spacious front porch to gain his trust. I would go back into the house and watch him through the screen door. Gradually, I was able to sit on a chair on the porch as he ate. It took about two months for Baxter to come up to me and rub his body against my leg. I purposely did not bend down to pet him as I did not want to startle him. Now Baxter comes when I call his name. He even jumps in my lap. It feels wonderful to have this shy outside cat voluntarily be affectionate toward me.

Take it as a compliment that Bubba follows you around and likes to cuddle. 🐾

Do Cats Have a Funny Bone?

One of my favorite humorists and cat fans is Dena Harris, "the Erma Bombeck of cat writers." The author of *Lessons in Stalking: Adjusting to Life with Cats,* Harris created this top 10 list (adapted below) of cat observations to show that our feline friends do indeed see some humor in sharing their lives with us.

- Our astonishing lack of hair

- The way we harbor the illusion that we stand even the smallest chance of winning a staring contest against them (Hint: Cats blink only because they feel sorry for us.)

- Our ability to pass through a sunbeam without dropping unconscious to the floor

- That we appear *not* to consider a live mouse the finest form of in-home entertainment

- The way we fold clothes warm from the dryer instead of diving headfirst into them

- The time we spend working to remove the glorious trail of cat hair from around the house when they know they can replace it all in 6.4 seconds

- That we think those decapitated rodents left on the back porch are presents for *us*

- That we ignore the primary uses of the computer and kitchen island, both of which are for napping

- That we choose *not* to walk around on top of the countertops, which is where all the best views are to be had, not to mention the treats

- Our never-ending devotion and eternal servitude to them (Actually, cats don't so much laugh at this last one as encourage it.)

GUILT-RIDDEN OR JUST PLAIN BORED?

Increased work demands have recently called for me to travel a lot more, and my cat, Keeper, a beautiful Bengal, is sometimes home alone for a night. I have friends who feed him if I am gone more than overnight, but he is still alone more than he used to be. When I came home from my last trip, he had shredded the toilet paper, clawed a corner of my couch, and tipped over a container of paper clips on my desk.

When I saw this, I marched up to him and yelled at him. He fled and hid under the bed for a while. Are cats capable of plotting revenge, and do they feel guilt when they do something we don't want them to do?

In the animal kingdom, humans have a monopoly on feeling guilty. Cats, dogs, and the rest of our animal companions do not experience or express guilt. It is tempting to anthropomorphize your cat, giving him human reasons for his misdeeds and for running away when you chastise him. But the truth is that guilt is self-reflective, an emotion only humans feel, according to top psychologists.

Guilt is a human response to behavior that we recognize as wrong or socially unacceptable. Cats do not have the capacity for that type of abstract thinking. However, cats are definitely capable of experiencing fear and sub-mission. It is easy to confuse feline fear with guilt.

In Keeper's case, he is most likely bored by those long stretches of being home alone. Bored cats, especially active breeds like Bengals, will look for ways to amuse themselves, even if those ways (turning toilet paper into confetti, clawing couches, and pawing piles of paper clips) are not desirable from your point of view. In other cats, these actions could illustrate separation anxiety. Whether a cat is bored or anxious depends on his temperament and relationship with his owner.

Keeper cowered and hid under the bed when you yelled because he was frightened of your angry voice, not because he was feeling guilty about his "bad" behavior. He had no idea why you were angry, only that you were acting scary and threatening.

My recommendation is to first take away feline temptations. When you're not home, shut the bathroom door, put a

covering on your couch to stop his claws, and tidy your desk. Next, provide Keeper with acceptable outlets for his boredom. These might include food puzzles, a sturdy window perch where he can keep tabs on the neighborhood, or a couple of motion-activated cat toys. Make your house feel more like a home by turning on the radio or television to add some sound to ease his solitude. There are videos of fish and birds and other cat-enticing images that might occupy his attention in your absence.

And for the times you need to be away for a night or more, consider hiring a professional pet sitter to make scheduled visits to feed Keeper, clean his litter box, and engage him in play-time. Organizations like the National Association of Professional Pet Sitters and Pet Sitters International have trained pet sitters who are licensed, insured, and bonded. They know pets and they give you peace of mind while you are traveling.

When you do come home from those business trips, ignore any messes and greet Keeper with happiness and affection. Spend some time playing with him and petting him so that he doesn't feel alone even with you back in the house. You may discover that he comes rushing up to greet you after an absence. 🐾

THE NEED TO KNEAD

Whenever I'm sitting down, my cat will climb in my lap, circle around, plop down, and busily start to push her paws (and claws) up and down on my legs. I call it her happy dance. She sometimes does the same thing on my bed before settling down for the night. Why does she do this?

The feline ritual of rhythmically pumping their paws up and down begins at birth. Newborns push their paws around their mother's nipples while they suckle to hasten the flow of milk. Even after they are weaned, kittens remember the happy feeling of a full belly that came with kneading and nursing.

As adults, "making biscuits," as I like to call it, brings them a sense of comfort. It is a way for cats to convey joy and delight at having you in their lives. If you regularly clip your cat's nails, you might avoid the pain of her nails plunging into your leg.

It's possible to go a little overboard, though. Some cats drool while kneading, and others become so enthusiastic that they drive their sharp claws into your legs. If your cat is turning you into a pincushion and regular nail clipping sessions aren't making it less painful for you, you can stop this behavior from becoming an unpleasant habit by simply standing up and walking away. After being ousted from your cozy lap a few times, your cat is apt to tone down her need to knead. 🐾

FOUR-LEGGED GYMNASTS

I am embarrassed to admit that I would sometimes hold my childhood cat belly-up over my head and let him fall. I was amazed at how he could twist his body and land on his four feet with ease. I have much more respect for cats as an adult, but I am still intrigued by their athleticism. How do cats manage to maneuver their bodies to land safely?

My advice is to never challenge a cat to a game of Twister. He will win every time, paws down. A flexible musculoskeletal system and a strong sense of balance enable airborne cats to right themselves rapidly and gracefully and, most times, safely. Their free-floating collarbones and supple backbones, which have five more vertebrae than humans, allow them to twist and turn in midair.

Their superior sense of balance and coordination comes from the vestibular apparatus, the fluid-filled canal in the ear that allows both humans and cats to remain upright when walking and to figure out where the ground is in relation to the body. When a cat falls, the fluid activates tiny hairs in the ear canal, allowing the cat to determine its body position and to identify which way is up.

Studies on falling cats have discovered that felines who fall from heights of 7 stories or fewer face greater injury than those falling from greater heights. In fact, cats have survived falls from as high as 18 stories. The explanation is that after falling 5 stories or so, a cat reaches terminal velocity. On a longer fall, it has time to right itself, relax its muscles, and spread out its limbs like a flying squirrel to slow down its rate of speed.

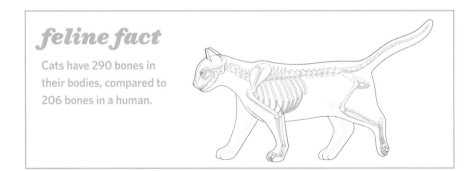

feline fact

Cats have 290 bones in their bodies, compared to 206 bones in a human.

The actual movements from the start of the fall to the four-on-the-floor finish are quite balletlike. First, the falling cat rotates its head and the front of its body to bring its legs underneath its body. The hind end then moves into alignment. Just as he lands, he brings the front legs closer to his face to absorb some of the impact and bends his back legs to prepare for the jolt.

As agile as cats are, they do not always land on their feet. Cats have suffered injury from falls off countertops and two-story balconies. That's why I strongly urge all cat owners to make sure that all window screens are sturdy and will not pop open from the weight of a cat perched on the sill. And don't let your cat roam unsupervised on a balcony. All it takes is one sparrow flying by and your bird-chasing cat could leap up and over the balcony ledge in determined pursuit. 🐾

CATS AND BIRDS AND MICE, OH MY!

In a *Brady Bunch*–style union, my new husband and I are trying to merge our teenagers as well as our cats, birds, and mice under one roof. We are optimistically hoping for harmony. I have two curious cats. He has one talkative bird and a handful of pet mice. He has never owned a cat. I have never owned a bird or mice. Can these different animals live in harmony with one another?

Many pets of different origins do get along, or at least tolerate one another. Some cats—especially those raised from kittenhood with birds or mice—can tone down their predatory nature and be friends. But you'll be a better friend to all your pets by keeping a close eye on their actions.

You can't erase the predatory nature in your cat, so if you wish to have a household filled with wings and fur, take extra precautions to keep mice and birds safely out of a curious cat's reach. Prevention is the key here. It is unlikely that your grown cats will come to regard their new housemates as anything but

potential meals. Even though some cats are not big hunters and would rather enjoy bowls of hand-delivered kibble, don't take the chance that the activity of the bird or mice might trigger an instinctive predatory response.

Even if your cats seem uninterested in the bird or the mice, never leave them unsupervised together. If no one in your merged family is available to watch over them, make sure that the bird and mice are safely in their cages out of paw's reach. You don't want a case of feline "fowl" play or a mouse murder in the house.

It is important, however, that you convey to your cats that the bird and mice are part of the family. Pay attention to signals from your cats that they are feeling more aggressive toward than amused by the smaller critters. Prey-focused cats tend to display overt curiosity. They may sit very still and stare fixedly at the prey or twitch their tails slightly and fold their ears back. Another big clue: Predators don't vocalize before they stalk and kill. Many cats, however, do make a distinctive chirping or cackling sound when they become aroused at the sight of birds.

Reward polite, acceptable behavior in your cats by praising them and offering them small treats when they are relaxed around the bird and mice. In general, I am not a big fan of remote punishment, but I am in favor of

keeping other pets safe. If one of your cats displays unwanted behavior, such as pawing at the birdcage or pacing around the mice container, you can toss a small pillow or squirt water near your cat to startle and distract him (don't actually hit him!). The message you want to deliver is that unpleasant things happen when he paws or stares at the caged critters. 🐾

feline fact

A cat named Stubbs, shown here, was the uncontested mayor of Talkeetna, a tiny town in Alaska, for 20 years.

The Top 10 Fabulous Felines

Sorry, canine pals, but in a North American pet popularity contest, cats win paws down. They also outnumber you in Europe. It's just a fact, Fido, that cats live in more homes than dogs do.

What do all these cats look like? About 95 percent of felines in homes are "just cats"—tabbies, tortoiseshells, tuxedos, and more, both short- and longhaired. Of the 45 pedigreed breeds recognized by The Cat Fanciers' Association, keepers of the world's largest cat registry, which ones rank as the most popular? According the latest CFA registration statistics, these were the most popular breeds in 2020.

1. The **Ragdoll** topped the popularity list in 2019 as well. Large and long-haired, the Ragdoll wins people over with its unusual coloring, big blue eyes, and mellow disposition.

2. The **Exotic** resembles a Persian except for its coat, which is dense, soft, plush, and medium length and does not require daily fussing. This breed is sometimes called the "Persian in pajamas." People love the Exotic's cherubic face, solid body, and calm, even temperament.

3. The all-American **Maine Coon** cat over-shadows most other breeds in terms of size and bulk but has a gentle giant temperament to match. This breed is often referred to as doglike in charac-ter. The long coat comes in a variety of beautiful colors, and you can't miss their gorgeously tufted ears.

4. The **Persian** has ranked as one of the most popular breeds worldwide since cat breed judging began in the late 1800s. This beautiful breed oozes affection. People love the Persian's easygoing nature and admire the long,

Ragdoll

Exotic

Maine Coon

Persian

silky fur that requires daily combing to keep it mat-free.

5. The **British Shorthair** sports a dense coat that comes in many colors, including blue, the most popular. These powerfully built cats are known as great hunters with loyal, pleasing personalities.

6. The **Devon Rex** is a dainty cat with a soft, wavy coat and large ears on a pointed face. Affectionate and friendly, they love to cuddle.

7. The active, intelligent **Abyssinian** loves to be around people. The Aby makes a perfect match for people looking for plenty of interaction with their feline pals. It is a regal beauty with a slightly rounded, wedge-shaped head, lithe body, and short, dense, silky coat, which is ticked like a wild rabbit and comes in several colorful shades.

8. The **American Shorthair** is a solidly built cat with a short, dense coat that comes in a wide array of gorgeous colors. This is a friendly and playful breed.

9. With its distinctive folded ears and round face, the **Scottish Fold** is in high demand. Not all kittens are born with the "right" ears, which makes this breed hard to find.

10. The **Sphynx** wins fans from among those who aren't hung up on a plush fur coat. What they lack in fur, they make up for with their affectionate personalities.

I love the look and predictable personality traits of the pedigreed cats, but keep an open mind when you think about adopting a kitten or a cat. Consider the spontaneous beauties of the feline world without a pedigree who are known by the abbreviations DSH (domestic shorthair) and DLH (domestic longhair).

British Shorthair

Devon Rex

Abyssinian

American Shorthair

Scottish Fold

Sphynx

CAT IS IN CLAW HEAVEN

I've always had fish and turtles and finally decided that I was ready for a more complicated, interactive pet. I recently adopted a big orange tabby from the local animal shelter. Gus is great, but he loves to claw and tear at his scratching post. Fortunately for me, he leaves my couch alone. Why does he have this need to scratch?

Bravo! With no disrespect toward the fish and turtles in your life, I'm glad you are ready to enjoy the perks of feline companionship. And I am happy that you have given a homeless cat another chance.

Scratching, as you have discovered, is one of the signature actions of cats. Even declawed cats will perform scratching gestures. You're lucky that Gus adores his scratching post and not your expensive sofa. Cats scratch for a couple of reasons. One reason is to keep their claws in shape—what I call a "peti-cure." Those scratching sessions remove the dead outer nail covering and hone the claw's shape and sharpness, keeping Gus prepared to defend himself or to pounce on a passing mouse.

However, the paramount reason cats scratch has to do with turf talk. When Gus scratches, he is leaving a feline business card, if you will. Scratching not only leaves physical marks but also the scratching action releases a scent from the sebaceous glands in his paws that communicates to other cats—and to himself—that this is his domain.

You mention that you are grateful he only scratches the cat post, but I bet if you pay close attention, you will discover that old Gus is also pawing and rubbing his face on doorways and wall corners. It eventually builds up as an oily discoloration on the walls and doors. He is demonstrating another common cat trait: scent marking. Think of Gus as a feline Zorro. When he rubs his cheeks and paw pads against walls, furniture, toys, and even you, he is marking these resources as belonging to him. Your name may be on the mortgage, but in his mind, the house belongs to Gus. 🐾

feline fact

Cats can be right- or left-pawed, with females tending to favor their right paws and males relying on their left paws.

INSIGHTS INTO CAT SHOWS

A friend of mine has a pair of Russian blue cats who she enters in cat shows. She has invited me to attend a show. I often watch dog shows on television, but I'm not at all sure how a cat show works. Can you give me some insight on what to expect and how to behave at a cat show?

Dogs aren't the only animals who like to mug for a camera or to strike a pose for a ribbon-awarding judge, and dog owners aren't the only people who like to show off their sleek, well-groomed, and highly pedigreed pets. You can learn a lot about cats by taking the time to attend a cat show.

Cat shows put the D in diversity. The Cat Fanciers' Association recognizes 45 pedigreed breeds as well as nonpedigreed companion cats. Attending a CFA cat show is a marvelous opportunity to see so many different types of cats under one roof. True, cats do not vary as much in size or looks as their canine counterparts, but there is a great distinction between a Sphynx and a Maine Coon or between an Ocicat and a Ragdoll. And I am glad that "mutt" cats like my

Casey and Rusty are also welcomed in the companion cats or household cat categories that celebrate nonpedigreed cats in the shows.

Most cat shows feature judging rings for seven different classes: kitten, championship, premiership, veteran, household pet, miscellaneous, and provisional. Like dogs, cats are judged not against each other but against a written breed standard of perfection. Rather than trotting around the ring in a group, cats are brought to a particular area to be handled and inspected individually by the judge for each class. Beyond the judging tables, you may also get to see cats compete in a feline sport rising in popularity: indoor agility. And cat shows also welcome young cat enthusiasts in their youth feline education programs.

For spectators, there is a certain etiquette required. Here are some inside tips I can share.

Never touch a cat without the owner's permission. Not all cats like being handled by strangers. Even the most outgoing cats can be startled or anxious if they smell another cat on a person's hands. You also don't want to risk passing germs from one cat to another or detracting from the cat's well-groomed appearance that took hours to achieve. Exhibitors will usually ask visitors to spray disinfectant/odor neutralizer on their hands before petting a cat.

Time your photo-taking opportunities. Ask permission before snapping away at a captivating cat being groomed or in the judging ring.

Don't engage in extended small talk with the cat show exhibitors. They are busy listening for their cats' numbers to be called to a judging ring and keeping their cats calm and well groomed. Ask if they have time to answer a question or two, but let them initiate any lengthy conversation about their cats and their particular breed characteristics. Most do enjoy talking about cats when the time is right. Look for exhibitors wearing "Ask Me" buttons, as these people are in the CFA Ambassador Program and they are always willing to answer questions or just "talk cats."

Leave your own feline friend at home. These shows are limited to cats competing for honors. And of course, no dogs are allowed! If you are interested in exhibiting your cat, you might be surprised to know that many cats, once exposed to the busy cat show environment, enjoy the process. And the experience boosts their social skills at the show as well as in your home.

I am also impressed that many cat show organizers work with local shelters and rescue groups to promote adoptions for cats in need of homes. 🐾

> ## *feline fact*
>
> The first cat show in the United States was held in 1895 at Madison Square Garden in New York City.

CHOOSING A KITTEN OR A CAT

I want to adopt a cat from my local shelter, but as a first-time pet owner, I need some advice. Should I adopt a kitten or a grown cat? What should I look for in deciding among so many? How can I make sure the cat is a good match for me?

These are important questions and you are wise to consider them before you bring a cat home. As you prepare to welcome a new feline into your life, my main advice is to think long term—you are likely to have this cat in your life much longer than you will have the car you drive. Sadly, people typically spend many hours picking out a vehicle they keep for 4 or 5 years but spend only a few minutes selecting a feline companion who may be part of their lives for 15 years or more.

You need to be honest about your lifestyle and personality and also be a bit selfish. Your new cat or kitten needs to match your lifestyle and your preferences. If you really want a shorthaired cat so you don't have to fuss over daily grooming, then please do not let a well-meaning friend talk you into adopting a longhaired cat, no matter how beautiful it is. If you like a cat to "talk back" at you, then seek out an active, chatty one, not a shy feline who likes to view the world from under the sofa. Do you admire an independent spirit or would you prefer a cuddly lap cat? An adorable kitten is hard to resist, but do you have the time and patience for the high-energy antics that come with it?

I recommend that you write out a checklist of what your dream cat looks like and acts like. Your mission: to seek a feline that best matches your list.

45

There are hundreds of cats in your area needing a home, so don't be in a hurry. Take your time and you will be rewarded with a lifelong cat pal. Visit different shelters and look in local papers for groups that rescue cats. There are also breed rescue groups to contact if a pedigreed cat would be a good match for desired temperament traits on the list.

Once you have assessed your needs, my advice is for you to be calm and passive in the shelter and to see which cat chooses you as a good match. I trust cat intuition. That's how my cat Casey picked me. He was among the cats from a local shelter on display at a Petco store. He immediately greeted me at the front of his module container. When I held him, he purred instantly. At 4 months old, he displayed a confidence far beyond his age. And he was very food motivated, even taking treats from me as a friend of mine paraded past with her well-mannered Border collie. I've always wanted a ginger cat because they have reputations for being friendly and outgoing, and Casey has certainly lived up to that.

Take your time and work with your local shelter or rescue group. Together, I am sure you will find the purr-fect companion. 🐾

Cat-Proofing Your House

Adopting a new cat or kitten is fun and exciting, but make sure you temper that enthusiasm with a dose of safety. Here are 10 ways to ensure your cat enjoys home safe home.

- Store antifreeze and other garage hazards away from your curious feline. One teaspoonful of antifreeze can be fatal.

- Install baby locks on cabinets where you keep household cleaners and other sprays. Be cautious when taking any medicines and pick up dropped pills so your pet won't mistakenly scarf one up.

- Keep thread, dental floss, and other types of string well out of reach. Many cats like to chew on string and may swallow long pieces of it. Some cats are also attracted to jewelry and shiny candy wrappers. Swallowing any of these can cause internal injuries.

- Inspect your window screens to make sure they are sturdy.

- Enclose electrical cords in PVC channels to keep chew-happy cats from harm.

- Put plants out of reach. Nibbled leaves can cause stomach upset or even intestinal blockage, and some are poisonous to cats. See Poisonous Plant Inventory, page 155.

- Keep your dryer door closed between laundry loads. Some cats like to nap in dark, warm places.

- Treat your furry housemate to cat trees and sturdy cat perches as alternatives to them jumping on your shelves and bookcases. Look around before you sit in a recliner or a rocking chair. A cat may be napping under the legs or inside the recliner.

- Block off areas behind heavy furniture, such as your refrigerator, couch, or a big bookcase—any place where your cat might become stuck.

COMMUNITY CAT OR LOST KITTY?

I just moved into a friendly neighborhood and have noticed several healthy-looking cats out and about. They don't have any collars or identification tags. Some also look like the tip of their left ear is missing. How can I tell if these cats are lost or homeless, and how can I help them?

A cat roaming around a neighborhood might be an indoor/outdoor cat who lives nearby and knows exactly where it's going, or it might be an indoor cat that has found itself in the scary outdoors and is lost. When there are several cats in the area, you might have a colony of community cats. These are typically felines born in the wild who have had little or no interaction with humans. The old term for community cats is *feral*.

In the past two decades, there has been a growing movement around the country called TNVR, which stands for Trap/Neuter/Vaccinate/Return. Shelters, rescue groups, and volunteers have a mission to humanely trap community cats, vaccinate them, spay or neuter them, and implant them with microchip identifications. The tip of one ear is cropped to identify that the cat has been treated, and then the cat is released to the same area where it was found.

It takes a lot of dedicated work, but these efforts help prevent community cats from overpopulating. One of my heroes is Paul Bates, community outreach TNVR coordinator at the Peggy Adams Rescue League in West Palm Beach, Florida. He spreads the word that these felines live outside 24/7, do not belong to anyone, and usually are not socialized with people. But they don't belong in animal shelters where they are often euthanized because they are not adoptable.

His advice when you see roaming cats in your neighborhood: Even if a cat seems like a friendly stray, do not attempt to pick him up and put him in a pet carrier. He might go into panic mode and try to scratch or bite you. It is far safer to set up humane traps to catch cats and transport them to a veterinary clinic that participates in TNVR.

If you are interested in helping community cats, I encourage you to contact a local cat rescue group or to see if there is a community cat department at your local animal shelter. They can help guide you on the right—and safe—way to help community cats live and thrive in their colonies. 🐾

True or False?

Feline fact and fiction have become quite entangled over the centuries. Here are some common cat "facts" that are actually fiction.

Cats eat grass to make themselves vomit. Cats do not necessarily eat grass because they have upset stomachs and need to vomit. Some cats actually like the taste and texture of certain grasses, especially broadleaf and coarse varieties. Grass also provides added fiber to help work out hairballs and added vitamins such as folic acid not found in meat. Sometimes a snack of grass does result in a mess on your carpet, though.

A fat cat is a happy cat. Just like us, overweight cats are at risk for a host of health problems. Specifically, they are prone to diabetes, liver problems, and arthritis. Keeping your cat at her ideal weight increases the chance that she will live a long, healthy life.

Milk is a healthy treat for cats. After kittens are weaned, their levels of lactase (the enzyme that helps with lactose digestion) drop by nearly 90 percent. That explains why many adult cats vomit or suffer from diarrhea if they ingest too much cow's milk. A spoonful or two every once in a while probably won't hurt, but milk isn't a necessary part of the feline diet. A better choice is a tablespoon of plain yogurt.

Communicating
with
YOUR CAT

We humans like to congratulate ourselves as being the world's best communicators because of our ability to talk. Some people speak several languages. Others wow us by delivering motivational speeches. But here's a reality check: Our cats "speak" much more clearly than we do.

Cats are straight talkers in their own fashion. They put the C in candor. They never deceive or pretend. They don't speak in slang terms or use sarcasm. If they feel threatened or angered, they hiss. If they are content, they purr. In cat-to-cat chat, there is rarely a communication miscue. The message is delivered clearly through body postures and a variety of vocalizations.

Communication between humans and cats often breaks down. What we may see as an act of defiance, like howling in the middle of the night or using the bathroom rug as a litter box, could be a call for help with a medical problem. We can't understand why cats flee from our hugs but often seem to seek out visitors with allergies or even an actual aversion to cats. We may not know the difference between a short, soft *mew* and a louder, elongated *meow*.

A cat dictionary does not yet exist, but we can have better communication with our cats by learning some of their "language." If we commit a feline faux "paw" or two along the way, that's all right. After all, to err is human, but to be a cat is divine.

HELLO, KITTY

I have some close friends who are self-described dog people. When they come to visit, they rush up to my cat, Pretzel, give him a loud hello, and then try to pick him up and hug him. As you can imagine, Pretzel is not a fan of this greeting. How can I tactfully train my friends on the right way to greet my cat?

You are correct in thinking that your friends need to understand that cats are not small dogs who purr. Although cats, like people, sport different temperaments and social skills, most are curious by nature. They rely on their keen sense of smell and their ability to read body posture cues when sizing up people to determine if they are safe or threatening.

Here's how to properly greet a cat.

- Ask your dog-loving friends to behave like "hush puppies" when they enter the room where your cat is. Encourage them to speak softly and to avoid making direct eye contact. Cats are not fans of being stared at.

- Ask them to sit quietly on the sofa and not make big movements or startling gestures. Tell them to ignore Pretzel and allow him to make the first moves.

- When Pretzel does approach one of your friends, remind them to let him make the initial contact. A cat may touch his nose against a person's leg, sniff a shoe, or boldly rub his body against the person. Encourage your friends to stay relaxed and breathe normally.

- Show them how to do the kitty hand-shake. Extend your index finger down to the cat's head level. Allow the cat to sniff your finger. He may allow you to stroke his cheek or he may lower his head and do an affectionate head bump to your finger.

- While it is tempting to do a victory dance and shout for joy, stay calm. Pay attention to the cat's body language. Make sure he has not stiffened his body or flattened his ears—signals that he is not feeling comfortable and may feel the need to flee or swat at you.

- And finally, let your doggy-minded friends toss treats for Pretzel to chase after and gobble up.

The bottom line is that cats take their sweet time in establishing connections and friendships with people. By playing it cool and by playing a little hard to get, your friends have a stronger chance at creating a long-lasting friendship with Pretzel that is based on trust. 🐾

TALK, TALK, TALK

My cat Maddie is extremely talkative. As soon as I get up in the morning, she starts meowing at me. If I *meow* back, she will answer me for as long as I am willing to play this game. My other cat, Whisper, is aptly named; he rarely talks. Why are some cats so talkative and others not?

Quite simply, some cats have more to say than others. Cats are a lot like people. There are the chatty types and the ones who prefer to listen more than to talk. You didn't mention if Maddie is a purebred or mixed, but some breeds are more prone to talking than are quieter breeds like the Persian or Maine Coon. Topping the chatty list is the Siamese.

Of course, there are exceptions to every rule. I've known some Siamese who seem to operate with the mute button on and some pushy Persians who never seem to stop talking unless they're at their food bowl or taking a nap.

Cats are quick studies. They realize we are only human and that we are often oblivious to their obvious body language. They make a range of pure and complex sounds with different meanings, and they often attempt to communicate with us vocally.

It sounds as though you enjoy your chat sessions with Maddie, so I recommend using those times to reinforce your special bond. Even if she doesn't understand explicitly what you are saying, she will welcome your friendly tones and the one-on-one attention. Behavior research conducted at the University of Bristol in England has shown that people who imitate their cats' playfulness enjoy better relationships with their cats. In addition, cats who are played with tend to be more outgoing, easy natured, and better socialized.

At the end of each day, it's not the words you speak that matter so much as it is your tone of voice and your willingness to spend quality time with Maddie. But don't ignore Whisper—just because he doesn't speak up doesn't mean he won't appreciate your attention and affection! 🐾

Cat Chat Deciphered

Some cats can be downright demanding while others speak only when spoken to. Whether your cat is a fast-talking feline or a quiet kitty, you have probably noticed that she has a wide range of vocalizations. You may be surprised to learn that cats are capable of making about 30 sounds, including at least 19 variations on the simple *meow*. Here are some of the most common feline sounds.

Mew. This pleasant, high-pitched sound is used to prompt people to do a cat's bidding, as in "Please refill the food bowl" or "Scratch under my chin." Kittens make this sound to their mothers when they want to nurse.

Meow. Think of the *meow* as a grown-up *mew*. This louder sound is made by adult cats toward people when they want you to pay attention to them or when they need to convey that their demands are not being met. Your cat is telling you that you forgot to feed him on time or that you absentmindedly locked his favorite toy in the closed bathroom. A series of meows is your cat's way to say, "Don't ignore me! I have demands!"

Chirp. This musical trill comes from the throat and ends in a question mark inflection. Momma cats chirp or trill to gather their kittens at nursing time. Directed to a favorite person, this sound might mean "I'm glad you're home" or "Oh, there you are" or "Please come closer and let's snuggle."

Cackle. Highly aroused cats often emit this *ka-ka-ka* chatter sound when they spot a bird outside on a nearby tree branch. Notice that your cat's lower jaw quivers as he cackles. It is a sound of frustration because the cat can't reach the bird. Do not attempt to touch a cat when he is doing this as you are apt to startle him and he may respond by swatting or biting.

Moan. This elongated wail of panic or protest comes from a cat who is extremely unhappy or in pain. Some cats make this sound when they are about to regurgitate a hairball or are trying to wiggle free when being restrained during a veterinary exam.

Hiss. It's not hard to interpret this one. Plain and simple, the heavy-on-the-S sound tells you to back off. This is an early warning sign before a cat feels the need to defend himself by nipping or swatting. An especially furious cat will make a spitting sound as well.

Growl. A cat who feels threatened or frightened will crouch down, maybe puff up his fur, flatten his ears against his head, and then snarl or growl. This is a warning sound to potential threats—new people, a strange dog, the cat next door, or even the veterinarian during a physical exam—to back off. Sometimes a growl immediately follows a hiss and maybe even spitting.

Yowl. Angry, agitated cats will often erupt into a screaming match if they feel threatened enough to attack. These screeches often precede or accompany actual physical contact. In a different context, a disoriented senile cat might yowl in confusion, as might a deaf cat who can't hear himself. Yowling after the death or departure of a beloved companion animal might be a sign of mourning. Female cats in heat will yowl incessantly, which is another good reason for spaying!

Shriek. This loud, high-pitched sound conveys that the cat is in pain or extremely afraid of someone or something. The mouth may be open and the cat's pupils may be fully dilated. Carefully assess for any physical signs, such as an open wound, limping, or swelling as well as any behavior clues, such as hiding, crouching, or remaining motionless.

Purr. This is a welcoming cat sound. Most of the time, cats purr when they are content; however, cats also purr when they are scared or in pain as a way to disguise weakness from perceived predators. So pay attention to what's happening in your surroundings when your cat starts to purr.

THE PURPOSE OF PURRING

My cat, Felix, loves to purr and does it quite loudly. All I have to do is pet him and he starts rumbling away. But my sister's cat, Ginger, hardly ever purrs, even though she seems to be happy and is quite pampered. I've heard a lot of different things about why cats purr. What's the real story?

The phenomenon of purring has fascinated humans for ages. And it is certainly one of the favorite feline sounds. My cat Casey purrs loudly and proudly. I jokingly say that he sounds like a Mack truck. In contrast, young Rusty is much like Ginger. I have to lightly put my finger on his throat to feel the purring vibrations that I cannot hear.

Purring is produced by the vibration of a cat's vocal cords when the cat inhales and exhales—and it's something they can do even when they are eating! It occurs at a frequency of 25 to 150 vibrations per second. Now that's quick! And it's a feat we can't imitate. In my classes, I offer $1 million (which I don't have) to anyone who can purr like a cat. It's a safe bet because people can only make purring sounds while exhaling, but never while inhaling. Try it for yourself. It is far easier to say "toy boat" 10 times rapidly than try to purr like a cat.

All domestic cats and most wild felids are born with the ability to purr. Felines, from young kittens to senior citizens, purr when they are happy, such as when they are being petted, anticipating dinner, or snuggling on a warm, cozy bed. Mother cats purr when nursing their kittens, and kittens purr when nursing.

Some cats, like my senior cat, Mikey, don't purr. It doesn't mean your cat is not happy or content. He just may prefer to converse through body language, facial expressions, and vocalizations.

New research from scientists at the University of Sussex in England indicates that the actual purrs made by cats can sound slightly different, depending on the circumstances. They studied recorded purrs and discovered that the purr sound is different when a cat wants to be petted than when it wants to be fed.

Many cats purr when they are afraid or in pain. That helps explain why females may purr during labor and why some cats purr when they are being examined at a veterinary clinic or when they are recovering from an injury. The purring might serve to reassure or comfort the frightened cat, and some studies suggest that the low-level vibrations of purring physically stimulate feline muscles and bones to keep them healthy and actually hasten the healing process.

Cats purr right to the end—when my beloved Samantha had to be euthanized due to liver disease several years ago, the sound of her purring comforted both of us as she slipped peacefully away in my arms. 🐾

THE HEALING POWER OF PURRING

When Sammy, my Maine Coon, saunters over to me, jumps into my lap, and starts to purr steadily, I feel the stress from my day melt away. I'm sure that stroking his soft fur and listening to his purring is good for my health, but is there any scientific proof of this?

Never underestimate the power of purring—scientists certainly respect that magical motoring sound. Recent studies have validated that hanging around a contented, purring cat can lower a person's blood pressure, conquer the feeling of loneliness, melt away s-t-r-e-s-s, and even bolster self-confidence.

About 68 percent of American households have cats, but it has only been in the past couple of decades that medical experts have conducted studies to validate what we always felt: Pets help us heal emotionally, physically, and mentally. Scientists are also discovering that cats and other cherished pets possess special healing powers that help people fight disease and cope with chronic conditions.

In his book *The Healing Power of Pets*, veterinarian Marty Becker describes the biochemical impact pets have on their owners' body chemistry. He interviewed numerous medical experts who provided the results of many scientific studies that support a biological basis for what we've felt intuitively—that people can be healthier by interacting positively and sharing their lives with pets.

A cat's purr stimulates our auditory nerves and provides us with a peaceful respite from the mechanical noises that are constantly bombarding our senses. Their vibrations aid in healing infections and swelling while promoting bone strength. And bonus: The purrs are soothing and free! No prescription required.

Try this the next time Sammy gets into a purr routine. Sit or stand and take deep breaths in and then exhale slowly. Just as in a yoga class, slowing down your breathing and breathing more deeply in sync with your purring cat can help you achieve calmness.

Some doctors even recommend "pet prescriptions" to their patients who live alone and need companionship. That's because physicians have discovered that a family pet can actually motivate some patients to give their best effort when dealing with serious illnesses such as cancer. Having a pet to care for and feed can stimulate ailing individuals to take better care of themselves.

Here are three easy and healthy ways to tap in to the healing power of your feline companion.

○ Spend some time each day just looking at, listening to, and talking with your cat. This releases those "feel-good" biochemicals that help you relax.

○ Rub your cat the right way. Learn to give your pet a therapeutic massage (see Petting with a Purpose, page 174) for some one-on-one time that will soothe both of you.

○ Engage in purposeful play with your cat and you might discover that you can let go of daily stress more easily, breathe more deeply, and laugh more freely. 🐾

---

feline fact

A cat's heart beats about twice as fast as a human heart, with a range of 110 to 140 beats per minute.

TAIL AS A MOOD BAROMETER

My cat, Noodles, was named for his very long tail. When I come home, he usually greets me with a sweet *meow* and hoists his tail lazily in the air. Then I hear him purring. My dog, Benny, races up to me to deliver doggy kisses while wagging his tail quickly from side to side. How do cats use their tails differently to communicate?

The versatile feline tail definitely does more than act as a rudder and provide balance. Like dogs, cats use their tails to signal their moods, sort of like those mood rings in the 1970s that would supposedly change colors when you were happy or mad. The key difference here is that a cat's tail position is far more reliable than those things!

Recognizing the messages delivered in tail talk can help you better communicate with your cat. Here are some key tail positions and what they mean.

Hoisted high. A confident, contented cat will hold her tail high in the air as she moves about her territory. A tail that is erect like a flagpole signals a happy mood or a friendly greeting. Cats often send this message as they approach a welcoming person. If the top third of the tail twitches as the cat nears you, this means that he totally adores you.

Question mark. A tail looking bent in a question mark often conveys a playful mood. This would be a good time to engage in a 5- or 10-minute play session.

Flying low. A tail positioned straight down, parallel to the legs, may represent an aggressive mood. Be wary. That said, there is an exception to this rule. Some breeds, such as Persians, Exotics, and Scottish Folds, normally tend to carry their tails lower than their backs.

Tucked away. A tail curved beneath the body signals fear or submission. Something is making that cat nervous.

"Hi, what's up?"

"Hey, want to play?"

Puffed up. A pipe cleaner of a tail reflects a severely agitated and frightened cat who is trying to look bigger to ward off danger.

Thrashing. A tail that whips rapidly back and forth indicates both fear and aggression. It is a warning to stay away. It is also known as lashing. By comparison, a dog who moves his tail side to side is often conveying a friendly greeting.

Swishing. A tail moving slowly from side to side usually means the cat is focused on an object. Cats often swish their tails right before they pounce on a toy mouse. It is part of their predatory positioning.

Twitching. A tail that twitches just at the tip is a sign of curiosity and excitement.

Corkscrew greeting. A tail lightly touching or wrapped around another cat is equivalent to a person casually putting her arm around a favorite pal. It conveys feline friendship. My cats Mikey and Casey show their feline friendship by lightly touching their tails as they pass one another in the hallway. 🐾

"That looks scary!"

"Best buds forever!"

THE HALLOWEEN POSE

Occasionally, my young cat will arch his back, puff out his hair, and bounce around the room on stiff legs. He looks ridiculous. I have to laugh when he strikes this classic Halloween cat spooky pose. Why does he do that?

Faced with a fight-or-flight predicament, a cat needs to deal with what he perceives to be a fearful situation. Inside your frightened cat, biochemicals are at work. Adrenaline starts coursing through his body. Special muscles also activate, causing his fur to stand up and his tail hair to puff out bigger. This is called piloerection. In addition, he will arch his back, flatten his ears, and spit or hiss loudly. Combined, these physical and vocal actions make the cat look like a poster image for scary Halloween movies.

Cats assume this pose to look physically bigger and more menacing to approaching threats. Notice that your cat also turns his body sideways toward the attacker to further magnify his appearance. Outwardly, the cat looks mean and ready to rumble, but inside, he is hoping that the attacker (be it a strange dog, unfamiliar houseguest, or

a startling sound on the television) will just go away and leave him alone.

This is a classic feline bluff posture. It may look comical to us, but this pose is an instinctive reaction to a perceived threat. If the posture doesn't work, the cat faces two other options: flee the scene or fight the danger. 🐾

feline fact

Although they ruled as world leaders and conquerors, Julius Caesar, Henri II, Charles XI, and Napoleon Bonaparte were afraid of cats.

EYE CANDY TIME

My cat, Dezzy, has beautiful, big, round, green eyes. She is a longhaired cat I adopted as a kitten about three years ago. She has developed into a very affectionate cat who likes to play and who follows me from room to room. Sometimes I try to engage in staring contests with her, but she always seems to break her stare and starts blinking at me. What is she trying to tell me?

Ah, you are the proud recipient of the happy feline eye flirt. Cats who gently and slowly open and close their eyes at selected people are conveying not only affection but also trust. Dezzy is telling you in candid cat language that she adores you. Make Dezzy's day by responding with soft winks back to her. She may be wowed by your cat savvy and display other forms of friendship toward you.

New research reveals that cats do not blink as often as we do. They also tend to squint more than completely shutting their eyes because of their inner hunter nature. If they shut their eyes, even for a half second, they may lose sight of prey they are stalking, which inside a home could be a fly that flew in or a toy you tossed down the hallway.

Dezzy may win your eye-to-eye contest because cats don't need to use their eyelids like we do to spread moisture on the eyes. They rely on their third eyelid, called the nictitating membrane, to keep debris off the eye surface. (See also Staring Eye to Eye, page 20.)

But do contact your veterinarian if Dezzy starts to blink excessively. It could indicate that she has something in her eye or is dealing with a medical condition such as a corneal ulcer, an eye infection, or glaucoma. 🐾

HOW DO CATS TALK TO EACH OTHER?

My three cats get along pretty well as far as I can tell. They don't hiss or spit at each other and they don't get into physical fights. I adopted them at different times, and they are now adults, ranging from 2 to 8 years old. How can I tell if they like or simply tolerate one another?

Cats communicate with one another primarily by body postures and scent marking and, to a lesser degree, vocalizations. Even though cats don't talk much to each other, pay attention when they do. Some cats hiss at feline housemates when they feel defensive or threatened, but that doesn't sound like the case with your crew.

How can you tell if two cats are buddies? Cat A may initiate a snuggle session with Cat B by purring softly and curling up next to him. Friendly cats may exchange soft blinks—a true sign of trust and affection. However, two cats engaged in nonblinking stares are conveying a possible feline showdown.

Feline friends often engage in mutual grooming sessions and may happily share napping spots. We have a cozy wicker basket on our living room coffee table that is big enough for one cat, but every night, Rusty sweetly tries to entice his big brother, Casey, to move over a bit so he can curl up next to him. Sometimes Casey welcomes the

company, and other times, he scoots out and heads for the sofa.

An important strategy for keeping the peace among cats in a household is to provide plenty of resources. These resources include attention from their favorite people as well as litter boxes, water and food bowls, cat trees, and bedding. Positioning these resources in separate locations can help reduce the likelihood of two cats sparring. For example, the litter box math is one litter box per cat plus one. In a three-cat household, four litter boxes in three locations is the ideal layout for minimizing stress.

Also recognize that cats tend to adopt a time-sharing approach for favorite locations. One cat may claim the sofa in the morning, a second cat takes over that spot in the afternoon, and a third uses it at night. In addition, cats need suitable outlets for predatory behavior. For the house cat, that means availability of toys to chase and pounce on. Food-dispensing toys also provide mental stimulation and encourage hunting.

Not all cats will cuddle together or play together, but that does not mean they aren't content to share a house. They simply have worked out a plan on how to peacefully coexist without being chums. There's no reason to force friendships between cats. When there is peace and harmony, why upset the situation? 🐾

HOW DO CATS PLAY?

My two dogs, Beau and Oliver, love to engage in a tug-of-war contest in the living room every night. Every morning, they enjoy chasing each other in our backyard. Their play signals are easy to spot. My two cats, Yin and Yang, seem to like each other, but how can I tell if they like to play together?

As you've noticed, dogs exhibit clear signals such as play bows and friendly yelps in their desire to play with another dog. It's trickier for a cat to know when another cat in the house wants to play. Animal behaviorists agree that there is not a well-recognized play signal between cats. One cat may pounce on the other and think it is in play, but the other cat may think it is an attack. To solicit play from another cat in the home, the cat may stalk the other cat, ambush him, hop sideways, often with the tail erect, and then retreat. Sometimes a cat will paw, bite, or attempt to wrestle with the other cat to initiate play.

Genuine play between two cats in the same house generally involves Cat A chasing Cat B and then Cat B chasing Cat A, typically without making any

feline fact

Sir Isaac Newton is often said to have invented the cat door, but Chaucer mentions a door with a cat hole in "The Miller's Tale" and there are examples of medieval doors with cat-size holes, so Sir Isaac just gets credit for explaining the principles of gravity.

sounds. Cats involved in play fighting usually do not move at a fast pace. They act more like wrestlers moving on a mat to get into position. But if the play begins to escalate into a fight, with more aggressive chasing and biting or yowling, you need to intervene safely.

Never attempt to pick up one of the cats during a fight. He might redirect his aggression to you by biting or clawing. Instead, call them or make a loud noise (clapping your hands or banging a pot) to stop a fight, or toss a small pillow near them. You can also drop a towel or blanket over the aggressor to give the other cat a chance to escape. 🐾

DARK CLOTHES, WHITE CAT

Every time I put on a pair of dark-colored dress slacks, I can count on my white cat, Toby, to enter the room and start rubbing against my legs. In no time, my slacks are covered in white hair from the knee down. I try gently pushing him away, but he persists. Why does he do this, and what can I do to stop him?

When a cat rubs against your leg or brushes his cheekbone against your hand, he is broadcasting two signals. The first is a form of feline flattery. You are the fortunate recipient of his affection. I know, flattery will get you nowhere, except, in this case, to the place where you stash the rolling tape to remove Toby's hairy signature from your dress slacks.

The second signal is all about turf protection. Cats have scent glands on their lips, chins, forehead, and tail. We can't smell the oily residue that is deposited from these glands, but other cats (and dogs) certainly can. When Toby rubs against your legs, he is alerting other critters to back off and respect "his" property.

By gently pushing Toby, you are unwittingly reinforcing his behavior. As you shoo him away from your legs, he enjoys the touch of your hand as well as leaving his business card on your slacks. Double victory!

It's clear that you treat Toby well and that he loves you. Perhaps a little compromise is in order. Create a bit of "Toby time" each day during which you give him some extra affection and sweet talk. Groom him regularly to remove some of his excess hair. Here's a grooming trick: Dampen your hand slightly and run it gently against the direction of your cat's coat. This removes dead hairs better than combing. You not only remove dead hairs (the only ones that cats shed) but also stimulate new hair growth.

A full bath or even a dry shampoo once in a while will also help keep the amount of loose hair more manageable. If Toby is overly insistent on rubbing against your legs, you can consider making your clothes less inviting. Lightly spray your pants with a cat-repellant spray or citronella (read the directions first to make sure they will not harm the fabric). One sniff and Toby will head the other way while you head out the door with clean clothes. But don't expect Toby to learn that it's okay to rub against your jeans but not your dress pants—you either have to accept a few hairs or discourage this display of affection entirely. 🐾

BOUNCE AND POUNCE

My 5-month-old kitten, Rex, often goes up to our old hound dog, Gus, and starts bouncing sideways. Gus looks at Rex like he just arrived from another planet. He does his best to ignore Rex, but Rex persists. He sometimes even paws at Gus's nose and then races away. What is going on?

Rex is extending an invitation to play. Kittens often arch their backs, puff up their tails (with the tips pointed down), and do a little sideways disco dance to pretend that they are being spooked. Obviously, Rex is in no real danger with Gus, but he may be in danger of being bored. He wants Gus to join in a friendly game of tag.

When we adopted Rusty, a then 6-month-old orange tabby, he immediately decided that Bujeau, our 90-pound Bernese mountain dog mix with a hard-to-resist fluffy tail, would be his best

play pal. I introduced them with Rusty inside his pet carrier next to Bujeau on the sofa. They got to sniff each other safely and to build trust slowly.

In no time, Rusty was leaping on our kitchen island at mealtime, waiting for Bujeau to start walking around the island with her tail high in the air so he could box at it with his front paws. I knew they were buds. Bujeau would intentionally make a couple of laps to give Rusty more time to play with her tempting tail.

Rex sounds like a delight, and he clearly needs more interactive play and some daily feline fun. Because old Gus is a no-go, I encourage you and the rest of your family to toss paper wads down hallways for Rex to pounce on or to drag a string for him to chase. He might like a game of laser tag on a wall. Just make sure that the area is free of breakable objects like your Aunt Dottie's antique vase. Be aware that even the most agile of kittens can misjudge and slam into an immobile piece of heavy furniture, possibly injuring himself and certainly bringing an end to playtime. 🐾

DEALING WITH DEAFNESS

I recently adopted Lizzy, a 5-month-old white kitten with two blue eyes, from a local shelter. At her first checkup, the veterinarian informed me that Lizzy is deaf. Of course, I plan to keep her, but how do I communicate with a deaf cat?

Lizzy is one lucky kitty to have you as her caretaker. Deaf cats do present some added challenges, but that just makes them more special.

Some cats are born deaf. A very brief lesson on genetics: Deafness is associated with the simple autosomal dominant white gene, especially in combination with blue eyes. The chance for deafness in white, blue-eyed kittens increases dramatically when both parents are white. Cats like Lizzy are more prone to deafness due to degeneration of the cochlear duct inside the ear. The mechanism responsible for pigmentation in the eyes also controls auditory development. When the pigment cells responsible for color are prematurely stopped, hearing is affected. What about blue-eyed Siamese cats, you may ask? They are never born deaf because they do not have the dominant white gene.

Other cats become deaf due to severe ear infections, drug toxicity, or head trauma. Old age is another cause. Whatever the cause, deaf cats are often easily startled, especially if you approach them from behind or nudge them while they are sleeping. Some deaf cats are quite vocal because they cannot hear their own voices and control the volume of their meows.

It should go without saying that for safety reasons, deaf cats need to live strictly indoors. I recommend that you microchip Lizzy and include an address tag on her collar indicating that she is deaf just in case she manages to slip outside. Attach a bell to her collar so you can keep tabs on her movements.

Because Lizzy can't hear you, you need to approach her face-first so as not to startle her; she might take a swipe at you out of fear. Approaching her directly

69

prepares her for interaction. Don't forget to ask your houseguests to do the same. If you need to awaken her, stomp the floor near her so she can feel the vibrations. If she is sleeping on a cat bed or piece of furniture, push on the surface next to her rather than touch her.

You can teach a deaf cat to come, sit, and perform other tricks using hand signals. You can also communicate by using a flashlight or laser pointer. Use the flashing light to guide your cat where you wish her to go. You can also employ flashing lights to distract a deaf cat who may be on a kitchen counter, clawing the couch, or committing another feline misdeed.

The bottom line is that with help, deaf cats can enjoy full, robust lives. They are remarkably adaptable and will compensate by relying more on their other senses, such as sight and smell. 🐾

WORD-WISE CAT

When I say the word *Treat*, my cat, Calvin, comes racing into the room. He loves taking short walks outside, and when I say *Walk*, he heads for the door where I keep his leash and harness. Can cats understand words the way dogs can?

Cats, just like dogs, deserve an A for being attentive listeners. They are masters at interpreting voice tones and body language and, to some degree, understanding the meaning behind certain words, especially their own names and that popular word *Treat*.

It is estimated that cats can comprehend up to 30 or so words. And even older cats can master the meaning of new words. A couple of years ago, I began declaring *Din-din time* to our cats and dogs before I headed to the kitchen to begin filling their food bowls. Our senior cat, Mikey, quickly learned that *Din-din time* is followed shortly by a bowl of food, so he goes right to the kitchen whenever I say that phrase.

Casey loves to cuddle under a quilt on my lap during the winter. When I say *Tent time*, his ears perk up and he heads over to the sofa so I can lift the quilt for him to crawl under and nestle on my legs for a cozy, comfy evening snooze.

Researchers at the University of Tokyo concluded that cats understand their names when you call them, but some choose to turn their heads toward you and stay in place and others choose not to respond. They are being, well, cats. The study also found that cats do recognize the voices of their favorite people.

How you say a word or phrase can yield different responses in cats. Here's a catty challenge for you. Without making any body gestures, make eye contact with Calvin and in a stern voice say, "What a good kitty you are. Let me give you some catnip." Then make eye contact and say in a cheery tone, "You are such a bad kitty. I hate when you scratch the furniture." My money is on Calvin being more apt to approach you when you speak in a happy voice than when you speak in a harsh, scolding tone.

The Name Game

One of the joys—and challenges—of adopting a new kitten or cat is coming up with an appropriate name. Some people are so conscientious about this that their new pets may go nameless for a few weeks until they discover the magical moniker.

Among the most popular cat names are Max, Samantha, Charlie, Gizmo, Buddy, Tigger, Lucy, Molly, Maggie, and Pumpkin. It is little surprise that more than half of all names bestowed on cats and dogs are human names or nicknames. This only serves to underline the fact that our pets have truly become part of our families.

Here is some advice on selecting names.

- Consider one- or two-syllable names because cats tend to respond better to short sounds.

- Pick a happy name like Muffin rather than an embarrassing one like Mr. Puddles.

- Avoid confusing your cat with names that sound like *No* or *Meow*.

- Observe your cat's behavior and personality and try to match it with a name. I know cats named Purr Machine, Kool Kat, Angel, and Love Bug.

- Resist the letter S, especially if you have a timid cat. Names like Sassy, Sadie, and Sasha, especially if spoken harshly, can come off as threatening hissing sounds to your cat.

HANDS OFF MY BELLY!

Alexis, my 1-year-old calico, doesn't mind when I scratch under her chin or give her head pets, but she definitely does not like me to rub her belly. I've had other cats and dogs who seem to beg to have their bellies rubbed. Why doesn't she like her belly touched?

I am not sure how long you have had Alexis, but calicos tend to be a bit apprehensive and cautious, especially in their younger years. A veterinarian friend once told me, "Calicos are a lot like chocolate. Sweet on the outside and nuts on the inside." He said it in jest, but it carried some truth. Whatever color the cat, however, the belly is one of the most vulnerable places on a cat's body, and many cats are wary of exposing this soft spot.

All felines need to become accustomed to being handled by people. Trust must be cultivated. For now, respect your cat's wishes and avoid belly rubs. Give her some time to become used to being handled by you and to learn that you won't foist unwanted attention on her. If Alexis strikes a belly-up pose and appears relaxed next to you, praise her, but don't touch her belly until you're sure she is inviting you to do so.

Instead, treat Alexis to some purposeful massage up and down her spine, using your finger and thumb (not your nails). Build up her confidence in you by petting her on her head and under her chin and welcoming her on your lap or by your side when you read or watch television.

Alexis may come around and turn into a cuddly love bug who will request that you shower her with friendly petting, even on her belly. If not, just understand that some cats have certain areas where they don't like being touched. 🐾

HOWLING AND YOWLING

I have two 6-year-old Siamese cats from the same litter, a neutered male named Kai and a spayed female named Kiki. Kiki behaves well, but not Kai. As soon as the sun goes down, Kai starts pacing the house and howling as loud as he can. I've tried quieting him by giving him attention when he seems upset, but no matter what I do, he keeps howling. I'm having trouble sleeping. How can I stifle this behavior?

Cats are naturally crepuscular, which means that they sleep a lot during the day and become more active at dusk and dawn. When the sun goes down, Kai has plenty of energy and he starts to pace and vocalize, perhaps out of frustration that he cannot join in various feline activities occurring outside.

Because his howling has escalated to the point that it has become a serious issue, the first step is to determine what is causing his hypervocalization. You may be able to blame genetics. After all, Siamese are predisposed to being big talkers. Increased howling may also be linked to Kai's need for attention or

it might have a medical cause. I advise you to have him examined by your veterinarian to rule out any hidden injury or illness causing him pain. Some cats become very vocal when they develop hyperthyroidism.

The cause of the yowling may be an emotional issue, such as anxiety or fear. Work with your veterinarian on selecting appropriate treatments or medications that can address these medical or emotional causes.

If you determine that his howling is just a demand for attention, you can extinguish his behavior by purposely ignoring his high-volume vocals. This won't be easy because initially Kai will probably howl louder and more frequently when he realizes you are not responding. When he starts up, do not say anything and resist the temptation to tell him to quiet down. Just leave the room or shut the door so that he can't see you.

At night, keep him out of your room and do not give even the slightest response, even to tell him to quiet down. You can start cueing him that you plan to ignore him by making a special sound like a duck cluck as you leave the room. This is known as a bridging stimulus and is employed to alert a cat that the owner is about to withdraw attention. The key is to be patient and to avoid punishment. After all, any attention, including scolding, is still attention in Kai's mind.

Another step is to tweak his feeding and sleeping schedules. If possible, play with him more during the day, which will cut down on his daytime napping and make him more tired at night. Provide his biggest meal at night, right before bedtime. A cat with a full belly is more apt to sleep than be active.

In some cases, a howling cat will settle down if tucked into a comfy crate at bedtime (large enough to include a litter box, with some room between it and the sleeping area) or placed in a spare room if you have one. This tactic does not work with all cats because they are not den animals like dogs, but some cats do seem to like having a cozy bedroom of their own. Just make sure that you make this a welcoming place with plush bedding and maybe a treat or a pinch of catnip and not a place of banishment. 🐾

A CASE OF NIP AND RUN

My cat, Peaches, is a Siamese mix. She loves to cuddle with me, but sometimes when I am petting her, she bites me. Occasionally it is hard enough to break the skin. Why does she bite, and can I train her not to bite after 12 years of living with me?

Peaches is biting the hand that feeds her, and without any apologies. It is easy to mistake the reason behind the nip. Peaches is not delivering a love bite, but rather a clear indication that she has endured enough of human kindness. Her nip translates into "Kindly stop petting me or I will bite harder."

Some cats bite because as kittens they were permitted to play "hand wrestling" with their owners, who considered it cute antics. They grow up thinking it is okay to bite and swat at hands. But when they do it as adults with big teeth and sharp claws, they aren't nearly as cute.

Other cats bite because they are scared or do not feel well, but because this has been going on her entire life, it sounds like a classic case of petting-induced aggression. While some cats can tolerate being petted, others feel overstimulated by the sensation

and automatically react by lashing out. Peaches is probably lashing out at you as a last resort after delivering what she believes to be clear prestrike warnings. These may include tail lashing, ear flicking, dilated pupils, shifting position, tensing muscles, and ceasing to purr. When Peaches displays these warning signals, that's your cue to stop petting. She has communicated to you in her best cat way that she is done with being petted.

I suggest you back off on petting Peaches for a while. Greet her in a friendly tone but avoid touching her for a couple of days. This will make her desire your physical attention. When you do pet her, do so for just a few seconds and then stop. By being better in tune with her body signals, you can stop before Peaches feels overwhelmed and save your hand from an unwanted bite. 🐾

BEATING UP THE POOR DOG

I never thought I would live to see the day that a cat would bully a dog. But unfortunately, that's the case in my household. My 3-year-old tabby, Roo, taunts, stalks, and even swipes at my dog, Tigger. Tigger is a 2-year-old male terrier mix who weighs about the same as the cat. Why does Roo badger Tigger, and what can I do to stop this behavior?

The real truth about cats and dogs is that dogs are not always the bullies. Some cats torment their canine roommates. It isn't about physical size but rather all about attitude. I've seen a cat send a German shepherd fleeing in fear. Bully cats like Roo want to control practically every situation. They may even

attempt to push their people around, too, by demanding meals when they want them and nipping hands when they decide they have received enough petting.

Bully cats do not accept punishment or corrections, but they do have a weak spot—they want attention. Use that to your advantage to help Tigger. Retraining a bossy feline is much like training a dominant dog. Start by exercising Roo more frequently to expend some of his excessive energy and to turn his attention to you as a playmate instead of poor Tigger. Protect your hands by engaging him in games with a fishing pole toy or cat teaser (a coiled wire with a small bundle of lightweight wood on one end that moves erratically, imitating the movement of a butterfly).

In regard to Tigger, the first step is to stop the attack. Look for early warning signs and stop a fight before it starts. Right before an attack, a cat will typically dip its head, arch its back end, and shimmy a bit. If you see this, try to remain calm. Scolding and high-pitched shrieks may only serve to fuel Roo's aggressiveness toward Tigger. Instead, step in and try distracting Roo with food treats or a favorite toy or spend a moment rubbing under his chin. Cats can't be happy and mad at the same time.

Separate the two when you cannot be around to supervise them. Avoid having them together during high-energy times such as mealtimes and when you arrive home. Reintroduce them when they are both tired, for instance, after you have played with Roo and taken Tigger for a brisk walk. When you do bring them together, keep Tigger on a leash and let him learn Roo's signals. It is far easier to rein in a leashed dog than to try to calm down an agitated—and agile—cat. Do this until you see that both pets are calm. Then unleash Tigger. Finally, regularly trim Roo's claws to minimize injuries to Tigger. 🐾

FEUDING FELINES

I have two cats younger than 2 years old who are not related. I adopted Abby first and brought home Buster two months later. Within the first day, they were buddies. But recently, Abby's attitude toward Buster turned hostile. I am now keeping them in different parts of the house.

When the door is accidentally opened, Abby will try to attack Buster, who hisses and runs away to hide. I love both cats dearly and wish they could be friends again. What can I do to restore the peace?

Cats are pros at hiding pain and discomfort. An underlying medical condition may be the cause of Abby's sudden temper outbursts, so my first piece of advice is that you have her examined by your veterinarian. It is not unusual, however, for cats who have coexisted peacefully to suddenly begin spatting. Try to pinpoint when Abby's behavior changed. This may be a case of redirected aggression.

Sometimes an indoor cat becomes upset or angry at the sight of a cat or other critter outside the window. Feeling frustrated, or perhaps threatened, the indoor cat will unleash her hostility on the closest target—usually another cat in the house. Or one cat will return from a veterinary visit and smell peculiar to her feline housemate who then responds by hissing or attacking this suddenly strange intruder.

Inside the home, cats tend to use a time-sharing approach for favorite locations. One cat may snooze on a favored armchair in the morning while the other one takes over that spot in the afternoon. A happy home can turn into a combat zone when there is a change in routine or when one cat, or both, feels the need to defend his claim on the shared turf.

You are taking the correct initial steps by separating Abby and Buster for their own safety and to reduce stress levels. Each cat should have all the feline amenities: a window for viewing, a litter box, food, water, treats, toys, and bedding. Every day, switch places, but leave their food bowls and litter boxes. These tactics get them used to the idea of living together and sharing places and objects.

Equally important is that you visit both cats. When you do, take a slightly damp washcloth and rub it over Abby's back, then on Buster, and back on Abby to share their scents. The goal is to swap scents with the hope they become more accepting of each other. While this is a common technique used to introduce two cats for the first time, it is also effective to get resident cats who are starting to feud to become reacquainted on friendlier, or at least tolerant, terms.

After several days, reintroduce them by cracking open the door to let them see one another but not be able to touch one another. After another few days, put a screen or tall baby gate in the doorway so that they can see one another more fully. If all goes well, confine the cats in a room, but place one of them in a crate and let the other roam freely. Then switch places.

If both continue to behave, you can gradually allow them to be in the house together. After any outbursts, however, go back a step or two to reinforce success. Reuniting Abby and Buster may take some time, so please be patient as you strive to restore peace. In extreme cases, you may need to consult a veterinarian about temporarily using mood-altering medications to decrease the level of aggression in Abby and the level of fear in Buster.

My parting advice is that you resist the temptation to coddle Buster or to shout at Abby. You may unintentionally reinforce his fear and her aggression. 🐾

feline fact

Famous cat fans include Leonardo da Vinci, Charles Dickens, Ernest Hemingway, Abraham Lincoln, Sir Winston Churchill, Sir Isaac Newton, and Florence Nightingale.

THE DREADED DOORBELL

My 2-year-old cat, Sugar, has always been a scaredy-cat. When our doorbell rings, she races out of sight. I'll find her under my bed or even under my bedspread. When I try to introduce her to visiting friends, Sugar tries desperately to wiggle out of my arms. Sometimes she has scratched my arms trying to escape. Why is she so scared, and what can I do to calm her down?

For the first four years of her life, my late great cat Callie pulled a disappearing act whenever guests arrived. Some of my friends didn't believe she existed! Like Callie, Sugar is exhibiting avoidance behavior in response to anything new in her environment, especially people. What causes some cats to be fearful while their littermates are outgoing is not known, but animal behaviorists identify several possible reasons.

Genetic predisposition. Some cats seem to be born reacting to new people, places, and objects with sheer fear. Even with gentle handling and positive experiences as kittens, some cats remain shy and a little standoffish with strangers.

Emulating mom's behavior. Kittens form habits by copying their mother between the ages of 4 and 8 weeks. If the mother is fearful of strangers, the kittens will learn to be afraid. Depending

Signs of Stress

Cats feeling stressed may exhibit any or all of the following behaviors:

- Excessive grooming

- Hiding

- Acting more aggressive

- Eating less or more than usual

- Suddenly skipping the litter box or spraying in the house

- Depression indicated by non-responsiveness and excessive sleeping

on the kitten's genetic predisposition, this initial shyness may go away with maturity and repeated good experiences with strangers.

Lack of socialization. The prime human socialization period for kittens is between 2 and 7 weeks of age. During this time, it is important for kittens to be handled by different people in pleasant ways. Undersocialized kittens are likely to be scared of strangers and may hiss, spit, strike out, or dash away.

Traumatic experiences. Cats at any age can develop scaredy-cat syndrome if they are exposed to a frightening situation such as being physically abused, lost, or attacked by a dog.

The more positive experiences you can offer Sugar with different people, places, and situations, the better she will adjust to future exposures. As you work to bolster Sugar's confidence, be patient and recognize that you will not convert your fleeing feline into a meet-and-greet cat overnight. Focus on small but steady steps of progress. Also be aware that you may never turn her into a party girl.

Because you know that visitors are the cause of her fright, recruit a couple of friends who are calm and who like cats. Ask them to come inside, sit quietly, and not seek out Sugar's attention. To keep Sugar from fleeing, put her in a room ahead of time where you can close the door and prevent her from dashing away and hiding. Then have your guests join you in the room with Sugar to watch a movie or to listen to soft music. The goal is to have Sugar see them and to realize they won't hurt her.

Build up positive associations for Sugar by having your guests offer treats. At first, place a bit of tasty cat food or a special kitty treat next to them so that she can approach without having to interact. You want to set Sugar up for success, and it will take time to desensitize her. Eventually, Sugar will realize that these people do not pursue her or try to pick her up. She may develop the confidence to approach them and actually take a treat that is offered. Let her make the decision to come closer and stop the experiment if she reacts fearfully.

Callie was a frightened cat for her first four years. But I knew she couldn't resist treats. I had my friends leave treats on the bottom of the stairs and move away so Callie could muster the courage to climb down and eat the treats. In her later years, she happily accepted treats out of their hands. Sugar may never become a lap cat to your guests, but these tips can help mitigate some of her fears and make her more comfortable in your home. 🐾

feline fact

Blessed with free-floating collarbones, cats are able to fit in tiny spaces such as boxes and dresser drawers left open.

CATS AND KIDS

We're planning to adopt a cat soon. Our kids, ages 7 and 10, have been pestering us for some time to let them have a pet, and they promise to help take care of a cat. They have friends with cats and enjoy playing with them. What can you recommend about safely introducing a cat to kids?

Growing up with a cat or any other cuddly pet certainly enhances a childhood. My first pet was a cat named Corky who joined our family when I was 8 years old. Corky loved to swim in our backyard lake with our two dogs. Four decades later, I still have vivid memories of that feline pal.

To prepare for your new family member, call for a family meeting to talk about the pros and cons of adopting a kitten or a cat. Kittens put the P in play and the D in destructiveness. During their first year, they explore their environment with reckless abandon. They grow up quickly, and your cute, friendly kitten might mature into a standoffish adult. If you adopt an adult cat at a shelter, you will have a better idea of his true personality, whether affectionate or aloof. Look for cats who can tolerate busy households with the television or stereo blaring, kids running up and down hallways, and people coming and going. Stay away from shy cats who may hide or become frightened by household hubbub.

Some pedigreed breeds enjoy reputations for being children friendly. Two good examples are the Abyssinian and the Maine Coon. Both thrive in noisy, energetic households.

Before you bring your new pet home, create a cat care schedule and post it on the refrigerator door or bulletin board. Everyone in the family should be assigned duties that can be checked off when they clean the litter box, provide fresh water, feed the cat, and groom the cat.

Educate your kids about the best ways to interact with cats. For example, cats do not like when people run up to them and smother them in bear hugs. A new cat may feel a bit unsure at first, so your children can help him feel at home by being quiet and gentle. Tell them to

sit and be still and let the cat approach them. When he does, have your children hold out their hands to allow the cat to sniff and rub up against.

Tell your children not to disturb a cat who is sleeping or using a litter box. He may feel startled or trapped and react by nipping or scratching them. Show them the right way to hold a cat by placing one hand or arm under the cat's front legs and supporting the hind legs with the other hand or arm. Tell them to be respectful when a cat starts to wiggle and wants to get down.

Most cats will not tolerate being dressed up or pushed in baby strollers, but there are always exceptions. If your new cat doesn't enjoy this sort of attention, your children need to know that there are other ways to play with their pet. Explain that they should never wrestle roughly with a cat or encourage a cat to swat and bite their fingers. Instead, have them use fishing pole–type cat toys or toss toy mice for the cat to chase and pounce on.

Finally, show them the right way to pet a cat and how to brush and comb the coat. Cats usually prefer to be stroked from head to tail, not patted on the head. Gently running a damp hand against the direction of the coat, however, removes dead hair and is a good way to pet and groom at the same time. These activities will help to strengthen the friendship between your children and their new pal. 🐾

DEALING WITH A FRISKY FIDO

Our 3-year-old cats, Kate and Allie, have very different personalities. Kate is outgoing, friendly, and easygoing. Allie is timid, a bit high-strung, and affectionate with us but not with our guests. Recently, we adopted a Labrador puppy named Marley. He is about 5 months old and extremely interested in the cats. He watches them all the time and wants to chase them.

Kate stands her ground and swats Marley on the nose. He immediately retreats. Allie, however, runs and hides when Marley approaches. How can I get Allie to stand up for herself and fight back?

Cats, like people, have many different personalities. Clearly, Kate and Allie have different attitudes toward playful puppies. Kate projects confidence and is actually teaching Marley what Aretha sings about: r-e-s-p-e-c-t. Kate is also teaching Marley some manners with a little tough love. Just make sure to trim her nails regularly because you don't want her to injure Marley with a sharp swat.

Unfortunately, those lessons are being contradicted by Allie's actions. As a result, you might have one confused pup. Allie lacks Kate's feeling of security and views this huge canine beast as a threat. Rather than stand paw to paw with him, she takes the fright-and-flee option and tries to disappear. It is not Allie's nature to stand and hold her ground.

The best time to introduce cats and dogs is when they are young. The first two or three months of life is the prime socialization period, a key time for cats and dogs to cultivate friendships. But it's not too late to work on Marley's cat-greeting skills and to bolster Allie's self-confidence.

Let's start with Marley. Labs tend to be fun loving and eager to please, so you have that working in your favor. Your mission is to teach Marley two important obedience commands, *Down* and *Stay,* so that he remains in place even when Allie enters the room.

To set him up for success, attach a long leash or clothesline to his collar to control his movement inside your home when you are around to supervise. Hold the other end or tie it to a heavy piece of furniture that can handle the muscle of a lunging Lab. When you are not home, keep Marley in a crate or in an area separated from the cats.

Keep a bag of treats handy. When Marley eyes Allie, redirect his attention by showing him a treat. Calmly instruct him to *Sit* or *Down* or *Stay*. Do not yell because you will only heighten his excitement and Allie's fearfulness. If Marley ignores the commands and the treat and starts to chase Allie, step on the line to halt his forward motion.

When Marley consistently demonstrates that he won't chase Allie, let him move around the house with his leash dragging behind him. If he starts to chase Allie, step on the line.

As for Allie, make sure that she has stress-free escape routes and dog-free zones. Clear out under your bed and provide a tall cat tree or wide, sturdy shelves for her to perch on out of Marley's reach. If possible, install baby gates in doorways of rooms where you keep your cats' food and water bowls and litter boxes.

Let Allie run to her safe spot when she feels threatened. Do not rush after her and try to shower her with kindness or sweet talk. These tactics only backfire by mistakenly conveying to Allie that she should be worried about this big dog. Act cool and speak in an upbeat tone.

Never force the two together. Cats feel most secure when they have "four on the floor" (all four paws touching the ground). Control the contact between them and go slow. Always maintain control of Marley and let Allie enter and leave the room freely.

Some dogs and cats can form close friendships. Others tolerate one another. As long as Allie feels safe—and Marley heeds your commands—life should get less fearful for Allie. 🐾

IS MY CAT SENILE?

My 17-year-old cat, Sammy, ambles around the house late at night, howling mournfully. Sometimes he wanders into a room during the day and just stands there looking confused. He used to greet his favorite visitors with a happy chirping sound, but now when they come up to him, he doesn't seem to recognize them. He used to love jumping in my lap, but now I have to bend down and pick him up. Alzheimer's disease is so cruel to people; can cats develop this condition, too?

On the outside, our felines often look younger than their physical years. But cats, sadly, are not immune to cognitive dysfunction. Some do indeed become senile in their senior years.

Our senior cat, Mikey, exhibits many of the behaviors you describe. Please do what I do for Mikey by having Sammy examined at least once a year, ideally every six months, by your veterinarian to rule out any possible underlying medical condition. Hyperthyroidism, liver disease, kidney disease, or urinary tract infection are examples of diseases that may cause hypervocalization or confusion. Some cats who become deaf also start yowling loudly.

Some cats start to exhibit certain telltale signs of cognitive dysfunction around age 12. Many animal behaviorists use the acronym DISH to refer to the symptoms and signs commonly associated with feline senility.

D is for disorientation. Cats who are disoriented often walk aimlessly, stare at walls, get "stuck" in corners, seem to be lost in their own home, or lose their balance and fall.

I is for interaction. Cats with impaired mental function often display changes in their interactions with people. They're less likely to greet people when they come home or to seek out a lap, as is the case with Sammy.

S is for sleep. Cats who once slept through the night may prowl restlessly, vocalizing as they roam.

H is for house-training. Proper bathroom habits often go by the wayside, not for medical reasons or displeasure with the state of a litter box, but because the cat just forgets to use it.

To ease the nighttime howling, try to break his daytime sleep cycle by frequently but gently waking him during the day. Or offer Sammy pieces of turkey or lactose-free milk at bedtime. Both contain tryptophan, an amino acid shown to possess sedative properties (which explains why you feel sleepy after a big Thanksgiving dinner). The idea is to make him more tired at night. Some golden oldies will snooze through the night if you treat them to a heated cozy or pad; look for one that plugs in at very low heat and has a washable cover. If these steps do not work, you could ask your veterinarian about giving your cat a safe dose of an over-the-counter antihistamine, which can cause drowsiness.

Try to stick to a routine as much as possible for Sammy. Add some extra litter boxes in different rooms and on each level of your home. This will help cut down on any "missed" litter box opportunities. Avoid litter boxes with covers, as old cats find it harder to get into them. Lower sides are best, too, as the hind legs are sometimes stiff.

Most important, shower Sammy with love. Spend plenty of time cuddling him and speaking to him in reassuring tones. Enjoy the time you have left with your ageless wonder. 🐾

Ageless Advice for Your Cat

Paws up to senior cats! Thanks to advances in veterinary medicine, improvements in nutrition, and stronger people-pet connections, our cats are living longer than they used to. Cats reach senior status by age 11, and those reaching their fifteenth birthdays and beyond are heralded as super seniors! Old age is not a disease—it is simply a stage in life. Here are ways to make your pet's senior years truly golden ones.

Ramp up the comfort level. Older pets spend more time snoozing—treat them to cushioned beds with egg-crate foam padding to curl up in. Add pet-safe heating elements to soothe their arthritic joints, especially during cold weather.

Don't be fooled by the label "senior" on commercial cat food. It's just a marketing term. Work with your veterinarian to select food that matches your aging cat's activity level, breed, and health condition. Spark a fading appetite by warming canned food in the microwave for a few seconds to release the aroma and/or adding a splash of sodium-free chicken broth to dry food.

Take a second look at pet-proofing your home. Reevaluate your home for a feline senior citizen. Place runners on tile and other smooth surfaces to provide traction for an arthritic cat. Keep a nightlight on in dark hallways to help a cat with fuzzy eyesight navigate better. Provide low-sided litter boxes on each level of your home for easy access.

Book twice-a-year senior wellness examinations. In the later stages of life, serious conditions can develop quickly but remain undetected without regular veterinary attention. I advocate super-senior physicals that include a head-to-tail exam, blood screen, urinalysis, fecal exam, and, if warranted, X-rays or an ultrasound. Catching conditions earlier means they can be treated more readily and with greater success (and often at a financial savings to you).

Keep life interesting! Provide senior cats with environmental enrichments to engage their attention. Tap in to their inner hunter by occasionally replacing the food bowl with a food puzzle. Keep playing games and tossing toys, but at an appropriate level of activity. Think about teaching an old cat new tricks. (See Click! Click! Train Your Tabby, page 208, and Top 10 Rules for Training Cats, page 210.) You never want to stop learning, and neither do your cats!

KITTY QUIRKS
and
Funny Felines

Face the feline facts. Cats *do* some unexpected things, but they are not rushing to provide explanations. And they definitely attempt—sometimes without success—to maintain their coveted dignity.

What we may think is weird, cats regard as normal behavior. Feline antics can be baffling, entertaining, and maybe a little frustrating to us, but they are never boring. Why do cats zoom up and down hallways like race car drivers? Why do some cats love licking plastic grocery bags? And why do some cats insist on saying hello by aiming their butts in our faces?

These and other cat antics have certainly captivated our attention. Cat videos and images have been viewed more than 26 billion times on YouTube channels and in posts on Facebook and Instagram. We love seeing cats fall off tables, jump into screen doors, and pounce on unsuspecting pups. There's even a website dedicated just to images of cats curled up in sinks.

It's time to take away the mysteries surrounding the feline mystique. That cat in your living room shares the same instinctual mindset as big cats roaming in jungles. All cats live to stalk, pounce, kill, and eat. All cats feel safest when they can survey their surroundings from up high, be it a tree branch or the top of your refrigerator. For millions of indoor cats, our homes are their jungles. Let's explore the world from your cat's perspective!

KITTY, REV YOUR ENGINE

I can almost set my watch to when my cat, Donny, will get a wild look in his eyes and then race around my house, leaping up on the cat tree, flying down the hallway, pouncing on my bed, and then scooting quickly into the kitchen. What causes these daily crazy outbursts?

Let me introduce you to feline zoomies, officially called FRAP (frenetic random activity periods) by animal behaviorists. This burst of high-energy action typically occurs once or twice a day among most indoor cats and, yes, at night when you are probably starting to fall into a deep sleep. Even though cats typically sleep or nap 17 to 18 hours a day, they need a way to burn off pent-up energy. Zoomies is how many cats prefer to do so.

Classic signs of FRAP include:

- High-speed bursts
- Arched back
- Eyes have a glinting look with dilated pupils
- Hair standing up on the back
- A sideways dance movement
- Leaping up
- Pouncing on toys or people or even the dog

Zoomies can be activated by a specific trigger, such as spotting an unreachable cardinal on a tree branch or discovering a new cat toy on the living room floor or suddenly noticing the wagging tail of your unsuspecting dog. Zoomies can also occur spontaneously as cats like your Donny suddenly feel the need to act like a four-legged acrobat. Remember, your cat is a hunter and has an innate need to stalk, chase, and pounce on prey, even if that prey is your pillow or a fly that found its way into your kitchen.

Age plays a factor, too. Kittens and young cats who zoom might benefit from more structured playtime with you and an enriching cat environment. When I adopted then 6-month-old Rusty, he had endless energy, so I set aside 10 minutes in the morning and early evening to teach him new tricks like sitting up and leaping onto a table, and I encouraged him to find treats hidden in food puzzle toys. I tossed paper wads down my hallway for him to chase and pounce on.

I established a comfy window ledge where he could watch birds and added another cat tree for him to explore. With the extra attention and enhanced cat habitat, he unleashed plenty of pent-up energy and I could sleep uninterrupted. Win-win!

Zoomies certainly can be comical and cute, but resist the temptation to try to step in and halt your cat by picking him up. He is in such a revved-up state that he may bite or scratch you. And if your cat seems to be increasing in the number of zoomies, please have him examined by your veterinarian for an underlying medical cause, such as hyperthyroidism. Sudden increases in activity levels along with losing weight and developing a big appetite are classic signs of this feline condition. Some older cats with dementia can also demonstrate senior versions of zoomies by pacing at night and meowing more. 🐾

feline fact

Household cats are capable of reaching speeds up to 30 miles per hour. Their wild cousin, the cheetah, can zoom up to 70 miles per hour.

MY CAT HAS A SINKING HABIT

No matter which of our three bathrooms I choose, my cat, Wanda, suddenly appears and scoots in just as I am closing the door. If I close the door to keep her out, she pokes her paws under the door or paws at it until I cave in and open it. She likes to plop in the sink, preventing me from washing my hands. And if I take a bubble bath, Wanda is perched on the bathtub ledge watching me. Why is she so obsessed with me in the bathroom?

Wanda, in her own quirky way, is displaying her affection and trust for you. She is choosing to follow you—not others in your family—into a small place, the bathroom. I know, we all need privacy at times, especially in the bathroom. But cats like Wanda aren't being rude. They see your bathroom occupation as a golden opportunity to spend one-on-one time with you. Cats also cannot stand closed doors. Their curious nature needs to know what is happening on the other side.

Cats are drawn to bathroom sinks for many reasons. For starters, they are elevated off the floor—making them safe spots. The smooth surface feels cool against a cat's coat. Most bathroom sinks are just the right size for a cat to happily curl up in to take a catnap. Some cats figure out that they can get fresh water to drink from a dripping faucet. Others genuinely enjoy playing with water and will dab at running water or pat the bubbles in your bath.

Wanda is not being rude by being in the sink when you need to wash your hands. Jumping into the sink puts her at eye level with you when you are on the throne. Just move her gently aside to wash your hands, then perhaps offer her a drink from the sink.

As for the bathtub, I agree that soaking in warm water is a great way to put life on pause. From Wanda's viewpoint, the bathtub ledge is wide enough to perch on and the cool tub surface provides a comfortable, calming feeling for her paws. She knows you are going to be there for a while, so she has you all to herself. She also is tuning in to your emotional state of relaxation. She can count on the tub being a place where you are quiet and still.

If Wanda happens to slip and fall into the bathtub, stay calm and keep still. She's probably panicking enough already and presenting you with paws full of claws. Grab a towel to dry her off and then give her time to restore her feline dignity (a big deal to cats) and to think about the best way to get up on the bathtub ledge without slipping. 🐾

PERPLEXED BY TAIL-CHASING CAT

My cat, Peanut, an 8-year-old domestic longhair, seems to have major arguments with her tail. She growls and hisses at it, sometimes bites it, and occasionally runs in circles after it. She also has been grooming herself to the point that she has bald spots on her coat.

If I intervene and pick her up, she gets agitated, wiggles out of my arms, and flees to another room. Do you have any ideas as to what may be causing this? What can I do to stop Peanut from bothering her tail and pulling out her hair?

Tail chasing may result from physical problems causing pain or discomfort in the tail area or, more rarely, it can be a behavioral problem (and yes, a weird one at that). In either case, this is a problem that requires professional intervention. Book an appointment with your veterinarian to rule out any possible injury to the tail, infection in the anal sac area, spinal cord problem, or neurological disease before regarding this as a behavior problem.

From your description, Peanut may be suffering from feline hyperesthesia, an extremely sensitive area of skin on the back, usually right in front of the tail. This complicated condition includes some compulsive and neurological behaviors. Typically, a cat with this condition will display dilated pupils, excessive skin rippling, and frenetic self-directed grooming that results in hair loss. The cat often targets the tail and flank area for over-the-top grooming.

Some cats become vocal and aggressive and may appear to hallucinate by acting afraid of their tail; sporting an excited, manic look; and fleeing the room. These cats are extremely sensitive to touch when they are experiencing these symptoms and may lash out at people trying to restrain them.

For unknown reasons, feline hyperesthesia episodes tend to occur more often in the early morning or in the evening. Aggressive behavior may appear spontaneously and for no apparent reason. Following an episode, the poor cat will appear confused.

Initially, some owners regard such behaviors displayed by their cats as cute or eye-catching. But when the problem starts to occur more frequently and for longer duration, it becomes a cause for real concern. Work with your veterinarian or behaviorist to pinpoint the situation that may have triggered Peanut's tail chasing. 🐾

STOP LICKING MY EARLOBE!

I have had Smokey, my 2-year-old cat, since he was 7 weeks old. He is very affectionate, but sometimes he insists on climbing up on me and licking my earlobes. He will even wrap his paws around my neck to get a better grip and then use his rough tongue on my earlobes—it hurts! I like cuddling with him, but I have to push him off me to make him quit. Why does he do this, and what can I do to make him stop?

Seven weeks is a very young age to be separated from the mother cat, so it might be that Smokey's behavior stems from being weaned too early. Smokey views you as his momma, and this suckling action on your earlobes mimics when he felt safe and snuggly while nursing his mother. A lot of undesirable feline habits start in kittenhood and are unintentionally reinforced by cat owners who view these actions as cute. In Smokey's mind, if you liked it when he did it as a kitten, why are you suddenly not such a big fan of feline grooming now that he has reached a hefty adult weight?

Licking earlobes may provide Smokey with a calming outlet. His desire to lick your earlobes is a signal that he trusts and loves you. Mutual grooming—called allogrooming—is an action reserved only between trusted friends, whether it's cat to cat, cat to dog, or in your case, cat to favorite person. Smokey adores you to the point of being obnoxious.

To stop his ear-fetish antics, you need to stand up and walk out of the room as soon as he climbs up on you, wraps his paws around your neck, and makes the move to lick your lobes. Don't yell at him or toss him roughly away; just put him on the floor and leave. By walking away, you are taking away attention, something Smokey obviously seeks from you.

Now comes part two of the plan. Wait a few minutes and then return. Perform an activity that you both enjoy. It may be engaging Smokey in chasing a feather wand, teaching him a trick, or tossing a favorite toy mouse down the hallway for him to pounce on. It is important that you don't just walk away, but that you give Smokey an appropriate alternative to socially interact with you. After all, you don't want to weaken that wonderful bond between the two of you. If Smokey persists, you need a last-resort tactic. Make a noise he doesn't like such as clapping your hands loudly or making a hissing sound. The idea is to startle Smokey, not harm or frighten him.

Also look for any clues that may point to a behavior disorder developing in Smokey. Changes in the home, such as the arrival of a new dog or the noise of construction on a new bathroom, can impact a cat's ability to cope. Make sure Smokey has plenty of cat amenities, including a cat tree, food puzzles, and toys. Consider plugging in a product called Feliway that emits calming feline pheromone smells our noses can't detect. 🐾

WOOL-SUCKING FETISH

My Siamese mix cat, Sake, is very doglike in many ways. He fetches toys, he walks on a leash, and he comes when called. As wonderful as he is, he has one habit I would love to break. He chews and sucks on any clothing made of wool. I sometimes find my wool socks saturated with slobber. It's disgusting. Why does he seem to like wool so much?

Sake sounds a lot like my first cat, Corky, who was also a Siamese. When I was in junior high, my grandmother gave me a beautiful charcoal-gray sweater vest. I loved it and wore it a lot. That is, until the day I came home and found Corky on my bed sucking on my vest. When I picked it up, there was a giant hole in the middle. I yelled at Corky, and he fled from the room.

Little did I know then that wool sucking is not unusual among certain breeds, especially Siamese and Siamese crosses. In fact, veterinary researchers have discovered a strong genetic pre-disposition for this odd fetish. Experts report that Siamese cats represent about 50 percent of the wool-sucking feline population, although the reasons for this remain unclear. Most cats stop this behavior by the time they are 2 years old.

In addition to the genetic predis-position of some cats, some felines are attracted to wool and other nonedible items like shoelaces because they may have been removed from their mothers before they were completely weaned. They seek out wool blankets and other fuzzy, comforting clothing as a way to compensate for their shortened nursing time.

Other explanations include dietary deficiencies—something your cat needs is missing from his diet. Ask your veterinarian about Sake's diet. Some wool-sucking felines fare better when they are fed a high-fiber dry food. The act of eating any type of nonedible is called pica.

Or he may be dealing with a medical issue, such as diabetes or feline leukemia. Once nutritional and medical issues have been ruled out, the cause may be behavioral. He may have a compulsive disorder.

In the case of a confirmed wool addict, prevention is the best cure. You need to make a conscious effort to keep all wool clothing out of Sake's sight and away from his mouth. Stash your socks and sweaters in drawers and put other wool clothing in closets with doors completely closed. During the winter months, make sure that Sake cannot reach any wool blankets on your bed.

Next, make the object of his desire less desirable, such as spraying perfume on your wool clothing. As tempting as it may be, do not make the mistake I made with Corky. Yelling at him will only cause him to be more anxious and be sneakier in his pursuit of the forbidden material.

Finally, give Sake some "brain teasers" such as having him hunt for his food by putting kibble in treat balls or scattering it throughout a room. Provide him with plenty of interactive toys in several different rooms. The goal is to increase his activity level and prolong his feeding time to distract him from other pursuits. 🐾

feline fact

A healthy temperature for a cat falls between 99.5° and 103°F (37.5° and 39.4°C).

CRAZY FOR PLASTIC BAGS

Every Saturday, I shop for groceries and place all the plastic bags on my kitchen island. Within seconds, Clancy is on the island rifling through the groceries, but he isn't trying to steal a cheese slice or chew through a package of hot dogs. He sticks his head inside a plastic bag and starts licking it. What is going on?

It's time to crack the case of the Plastic Bag Feline Attraction. My cat, Rusty, does the same thing as we unload our groceries. This feline attraction to plastic bags has puzzled veterinarians and behaviorists for many years. Here are three possible explanations.

○ Plastic bags are often made with animal fat or fish oils that keep the plastic from sticking together. The bags also carry the scent of groceries, like cheese and meat. The feline nose can easily detect those protein aromas, so why not have a taste?

○ Cats may like the sound plastic bags make when they paw at them or even climb inside. That crinkly sound may mimic the sound a stalked mouse makes, bringing out the hunter in your cat. For some cats, it is an irresistible cue to pounce.

○ Another reason may be due to pica, which is an urge to eat nonfood items. (See Wool-Sucking Fetish, page 96.)

Bottom line: Do not leave plastic bags out for cats to investigate. These bags can be choking hazards, and can cause intestinal obstruction or lead to suffocation. The best solution, for Clancy and for the planet, is to switch to reusable bags that offer less temptation for tasting. 🐾

COUNTER COMMANDOES

When I come home in the evening, I always have to shoo Salt and Pepper, my pair of gray-and-white tabbies, off my kitchen counters. I hate the thought of their litter-coated paws walking on counters where I do my food preparation. It's embarrassing when guests witness my cats jumping on the counters. They are great cats in so many other ways, but how can I break them of this disgusting habit?

Salt and Pepper do belong in the kitchen, but in your spice rack and not as a pair of felines on the counters. Feline counter surfing is an annoyance for many people. I agree that it is unappetizing to think of dirty paws trespassing on eating surfaces. It can also be dangerous. A curious cat can leap up on a hot stove, land on a knife, or knock a glass to the floor.

To keep your nimble felines off these places, you need to understand why they jump up there in the first place. Put yourself in their paws. The counter is high. Cats love to survey the scene from a safe and elevated perch. And kitchen counters offer an added bonus: They smell good. Even after a good scrubbing, counters still smell like broiled chicken, tuna casserole, or grilled steaks to cruising cats. Salt and Pepper may be hoping to find some bits of leftover food not captured by your cleanup sponge.

My young ginger cat, Rusty, is quite a feline foodie. His motto is, "Have nose, must find morsels!" At dinnertime, we fill our plates and go with two options, depending on the amount of food in pots and bowls. We temporarily place the extra food in our microwave or oven while we eat. Or we usher Rusty in a relaxed way into our bedroom where he can view squirrels and birds from his cat tree by the window. We let him out after we have cleaned the kitchen.

To retrain your counter duo, make the dining room table and kitchen counters less appealing and up the feline real estate value elsewhere. Start by placing double-sided tape on the edge of your counters and dining room table. Cats detest the feel of sticky tape on their paws. A good way to do this without having to pull up the tape when you want to cook or eat is to put double-sided tape on placemats and position them all over your counters.

Or buy an inexpensive office chair mat that has a nubby bottom to prevent slippage. Cut it to fit and place nubby side up on the counters to make it an unpleasant feel on cat paws. A third tactic is to use cleaners on your counters that contain citrus, an aroma cats hate.

Accommodate your cats' need to be up high by offering them a sturdy, tall cat tree in a high-traffic place such as your living room. This location allows Salt and Pepper to check out all the household activities from a lofty perch. Entice your cats to use this cat tree by sprinkling some catnip on it and serving their meals and dishing out treats on the different tree levels. 🐾

YOU'RE PLAYING MY (SAFE) SONG

My cat, Lola, is extremely fearful during thunderstorms or even with loud noises in our home. She sometimes yowls loudly, resists being held, and does her best to race to a safe place, like the back of my bedroom closet. She trembles until the storm passes. I don't want to add to her fright. I've heard that certain music may help calm cats. Is that true? If so, what type of music works best?

Noise phobia is a real issue in some cats and dogs. They can pick up sounds at higher and lower frequencies than we can. During a thunderstorm, some cats can turn into panic puddles because they hear the loud wind noise, feel the change in static barometric pressure, and may even see large trees bending over.

I am glad that you are seeking ways to help Lola. Unaddressed, the fear of specific sounds can escalate to a phobia, an exaggerated, irrational response that can emotionally and physically affect your cat. Some scared cats can suffer inflammatory bowel disease or weakened immune systems or may display unwanted behaviors such as fear biting or swatting.

To counter the noise from the storm, play calming music for Lola. Music can minimize pain, decrease anxiety, and serve as a powerful distraction for people and pets. Music does indeed help some anxious or frightened cats to calm down, relax, and eventually go to sleep. Possible benefits include lower heart rates and blood pressure levels, slower breathing, elevated endorphin levels, and decreased stress hormones. Music experts and animal behaviorists have discovered that the most calming types of music for cats include classical, reggae, and soft rock.

You may also turn on a white-noise machine or put a fan on high speed to help muffle the storm's sound. You can also purchase pheromone sprays or plug-ins made to bring a sense of calm to cats. Consider discussing supplement and medication options with your veterinarian. Popular choices include supplements containing zylkene, a milk protein that has calming properties, or antianxiety prescription medicine to give before a forecast storm arrives.

Finally, keep giving Lola access to safe hiding places such as your bedroom closet. Do not attempt to pick her up and hug her. Your good intentions can send her into fight-or-flee mode and you could get scratched or bitten. 🐾

Music That's the Cat's Meow

Music just for felines? Really? That's exactly what David Teie, a cello soloist with the National Symphony Orchestra, set out to create, using sounds that have meaning for cats, like purring and birds chirping. With more than a decade of anecdotal evidence and a few scientific studies, it seems clear that cats prefer music made for them.

In a study conducted at Louisiana State University's School of Veterinary Medicine, cats who heard feline-specific music were calmer and less stressed during and after visits to clinics, compared to cats who heard classical music or silence. Learn more at musicforcats.com.

HOLY TISSUE TERROR

It's a good thing that toilet paper and tissues are inexpensive. Our gray tabby, Abigail, seems to get a big kick out of rolling all the paper off the toilet roll and stealing tissues from the box and shredding them into tiny pieces. We try to remember to close the bathroom door when we leave, but Abigail seizes any opportunity to destroy our paper products. Any explanations and suggestions?

Some cats just hate being bored and will make their own fun if they need to. Clearly, Abigail needs more playtime and more stimulating games to focus her attention and energy. She is also searching for outlets for her need to hunt. Let me offer you a few remedies to help when you forget to close the bathroom door.

- Turn the tissue boxes upside down when not in use, making it much harder for Abigail to snatch a tissue and start shredding.

- Hide the tissue box inside a decorative basket.

- Install a toilet roll dispenser that covers the top of the toilet roll and prevents paws from grabbing the end of the sheet and unraveling the roll.

Now that you have come up with a game plan for your bathroom, it's time to work on diverting Abigail's attention to a more acceptable item to shred. Offer her food puzzles to test her hunting skills and to work her brain. Schedule mini-playtimes with her—5 to 10 minutes—and engage her with a feather toy or other activity. If you know that Abigail is a paper shredder and not a paper eater, offer her a cardboard box that contains crumpled-up paper for her to play with far away from the bathroom. 🐾

UGH, DEAD BUG!

My cat, Lucy, should be called Shadow. She loves following me from room to room. She jumps up on my lap and takes naps. She really enjoys sleeping on the bed with me. But once in a while, I discover a dead bug on my pillow. Ugh. I want to scold Lucy, but she looks at me with such pride. Why is she doing this?

Cats have novel ways of showing that they love us and that they are worthy hunters. Many of my cats have presented me with "gifts"—dead crickets, lizards, and bugs on my pillow and kitchen counter.

Lucy is demonstrating a classic cat trait. She needs to hunt. It's hardwired in her brain. Some cats kill prey that dares to wander inside our homes with plans to snack later, but others just leave the carcass lying around. Cats who are bonded to their people—as Lucy is to you—are bringing these "gifts" in an effort to train us. Perhaps they have

realized what lousy hunters we are. Or maybe they do it because they want our approval. They can't go out and buy expensive gifts on charge cards, so they hunt and offer us what they view as valued presents.

As disgusting as these pillow prizes are, don't make a big deal out of removing them because you know Lucy is watching you and waiting for a reaction. As an alternative, offer Lucy some fake prey to stalk and chase in your home, such as battery-operated toy mice that move erratically. Happy hunting! 🐾

CRAZY FOR CATNIP

I hope you can settle a family bet. I say that all cats react to the smell of catnip, but my husband insists that they don't. Our cat, Gigi, comes running when I sprinkle fresh catnip on her cat tree. She races up the tree and starts rolling in the catnip and eating it. She loves it. But my husband had a cat who totally ignored catnip. When it comes to catnip, what's the deal with cats?

I hope you didn't bet money with your husband because he wins this friendly bet. Cats of all sizes, from domesticated tabbies to mountain lions, have been known to roll over, rub their faces, and twist their bodies in patches of this aromatic herb. Researchers report that up to 70 percent of cats exposed to catnip display some type of reaction and that the level of response appears to be influenced by genetics. Kittens don't appreciate catnip until they are at least 6 weeks old, and about 30 percent

of adult cats show no reaction at all. Different cats, even ones from the same litter, can display different responses to catnip, ranging from no reaction to total bliss to irritability.

Catnip (*Nepeta cataria*) is a member of the mint family. The volatile oil from catnip leaves contains a chemical called nepetalactone, the odor of which closely resembles a substance present in a female cat's urine. Yuck. But these oils enter a cat's smell receptors in the nose and then trigger a response in the part of the cat's brain that regulates emotional responses. Most cats will rub their chins and cheeks or roll their entire bodies in catnip, while some cats also lick and chew it. The effects last, on average, from 5 to 15 minutes.

A pinch or two of fresh or dried catnip is enough to bring out the wild antics in your cat. It is interesting to note that this psychosexual response cannot be triggered again for at least another hour after the first exposure to catnip. For some reason, cats need some time between servings of catnip to reset

Three Catnip Alternatives

If your cat turns up his nose at catnip, try offering him toys filled with silver vine, Tatarian honeysuckle, or valerian root. You can find them in pet supply stores and online. Scientists have no explanation for why about 30 percent of cats who show no reaction to catnip seem to respond to these aromas.

Silver vine is a climbing plant that contains two feline attractants: nepetalactone and actinidine, making it more potent than catnip. Actinidine is also found in valerian root, causing some cats to flop around and be in high play mode when they detect this strong smell. A few even drool with delight. The Tatarian honeysuckle shrub elicits a similar although less intense reaction than catnip. You must moisten the honeysuckle to activate its odor.

silver vine

Tatarian honeysuckle

valerian root

their senses. Offer your cats some catnip about 20 minutes before bedtime. The herb should stimulate them to do enough exercise to become sufficiently tired to sleep through the night.

I recommend that you treat your cat to toys filled with organic catnip, the highest quality of this feline-favorite herb. Store loose catnip in an airtight, dry container out of direct sunlight. Do not keep catnip in the refrigerator because the cold and damp will weaken the herb's potency.

You might try making a cup of freshly steeped catnip tea for yourself. For humans, catnip works as a sedative, not a stimulant, making it a perfect choice to help us fall into dreamland. 🐾

FUNNY-FACE FELINE

What is happening with my cat, Mambo? On occasion, he seems to get into a hypnotic state when he sniffs something very intently. He opens his mouth slightly, wrinkles his nose, grimaces, and curls back his lips.

It is such a strange-looking pose. It usually happens when he smells some bushes. I've never seen him do it in the house. Is this something only cats do, and why?

Mambo is exhibiting the flehmen response. That funny face is not limited to cats. Many other mammals, including lions, bats, and horses, strike this pose in response to particular smells. Mambo's nose is alerting him to possible female cats in heat or male trespassers in the neighborhood. The interesting scent in this case is urine.

The scientific explanation is that as Mambo draws in air, he sends the odor through a specialized sac known as Jacobson's organ or the vomeronasal organ. This organ is located in the roof of the mouth, where it traps odor molecules and dispatches information to the brain. Flehmen can occur with many scents, but it generally happens when an animal—male or female—smells urine.

Mambo is pinning down phero-mones, chemical substances generated by animals that serve as a form of aromatic communication. With one deep sniff Mambo can access all sorts of information about another animal as if that critter left a business card. He can assess the gender, reproductive status, and health of other animals who left their marks behind. If you want to get the real lowdown on neighborhood gossip, then Mambo's nose truly knows! 🐾

LAP OF LUXURY

All the cats I've had before Jessie were content with sitting next to me or near me. Not Jessie. She insists on climbing into my lap and settling down and purring. She is very quick. Often when I sit down, she comes out of nowhere a few seconds later and leaps into my lap. She can sit anywhere. Why does she want to be in my lap all the time?

Exercise-minded people are always checking their Fitbits to calculate how many steps they take in a day. Cats, on the other hand, are fans of what I call Sitbits. They love to seek and find places of comfort.

My senior cat, Mikey, is like Jessie. Cats who like to cuddle view laps as triple delights. First, laps are elevated. Cats like to roost up off the floor where they can survey the activities around them. Second, laps are warm. Our body heat attracts cats, especially during the colder months. Third, laps are safe. Snuggling with a favorite person, a cat enjoys a sense of security.

Some cats take advantage of their one-on-one moments with you to dig their claws in a rhythmic motion up and down (ouch!) on your legs. Kneading helps them relive those glory kitten days when they nursed on their mothers and felt totally safe and secure (see The Need to Knead, page 35). You might enjoy this bonding time more if you trim your cat's nails or place a folded blanket or towel across your lap to protect your thighs.

Count yourself fortunate you have a lovable lap-seeking feline friend in Jessie. Her presence in your lap can serve to bring you feelings of contentment and relaxation as well. 🐾

THE CAT-CRINKLE CONNECTION

My cat can be snoozing, but if I take a piece of paper or cellophane or foil and form it into a wad, she instantly wakes up and is ready for a hunt. She loves crinkly sounds and will run after a paper ball if I toss it down the hallway. If I rattle a paper grocery bag and leave it on the floor, she comes running and will jump inside the bag. What's the big attraction of crinkly-sounding objects for cats?

Even though these everyday household items are inanimate, the crinkling sounds they produce mimic the high-pitched chatter of birds, crickets, mice, and rats, thereby triggering a cat's predatory response. Your cat's imagination is fully engaged as she pretends these items are the real deal. You are giving her the chance to hone her hunting skills and to show off a bit in front of you.

Some cats show a similar interest in shiny objects. Oddly, specific breeds, including the Manx, Japanese Bobtail, and Munchkin, have a tendency to collect and hoard glittery objects, such as jewelry and silver coins, and to stash them in strange places such as inside a shoe or underneath a recliner.

MY BIG FAT CAT BUTT

My cat, JJ, instantly raises his butt and tail high in the air whenever I pet him or scratch his back. It's obvious that he enjoys the contact. He doesn't seem to mind that he is "mooning" me with his rear end. Why does he do this, and can I get him to stop?

JJ is demonstrating what's known among feline fans as "elevator butt." You push the right button by scratching just the right spot, and he can't help but raise his butt up high. After all, he has been doing it since birth.

Kittens raise their back ends and hoist their tails high for their mothers to inspect and clean. This early stimulation was both functional and pleasurable. Now as an adult, JJ's so-called mooning is just his way of telling you that you are worthy of scratching a sensitive area that feels good to him.

In addition, when cats stick their butts in our faces, it is a form of social greeting. After all, friendly cats like to exchange scents, and where else is there a stronger scent source than a cat's butt?

Stopping JJ's hardwired behavior would be like trying to keep your eyes open when you sneeze. It's impossible. Just relax and appreciate his enjoyment of your attention. If he performs this in front of company (and you know he will), let humor be your guide and simply declare that it is "elevator butt" time. If it embarrasses you, don't scratch his back in front of your guests! 🐾

Many, Many Toes

Count the number of toes on your cat's front paw—it should total five. Now check the back paw—you should count four toes. Some cats, however, sport as many as seven toes on each paw. Having extra toes, or being polydactyl, is a congenital abnormality but not a health concern. Any feline breed can sport extra toes on the front and/or back paws.

Legend has it that seventeenth-century sailors regarded polydactyl cats as lucky, because the added toes made them better hunters and gave them better balance on ships during rocky weather.

In Key West, Florida, there is a major tourist attraction for cat fans. Dozens of polydactyl cats roam the grounds of the home of the late great writer (and cat lover) Ernest Hemingway. All of these cats are well cared for and even protected by terms of his will. That explains why polydactyl cats are sometimes nicknamed "Hemingway cats." Other admirers call them "thumb cats" or "mitten cats."

The world record for the most toes belongs to a cat named Tiger who had 27 toes and lived in Alberta, Canada. His prodigious digits landed him in the 2002 *Guinness Book of World Records*.

SAVING FACE AFTER A FALL

I know cats are very agile and possess great balance. So I have to laugh when my cat, Chandler, misjudges the distance to a window ledge, leaps, misses, and hits the ground. It's not far, and he never gets hurt.

Whenever it happens, he immediately launches into grooming himself. Chandler is a shorthaired black-and-white cat, about 4 years old. His coat always looks shiny and clean. Why does he groom after he falls?

Cats are dignified sentient beings. While they often act playful or even silly, they are easily discomforted by unexpected events or surprises. Many people notice that their cats will quickly turn away from a startling experience and begin mini-grooming sessions. For cats, grooming has important functions beyond health and cleanliness. The many benefits of grooming began at birth. Mother cats meticulously clean their kittens. That vigorous licking imparts the power of touch and strengthens the emotional connection between mother and kitten. Littermates often groom each other as a way to develop their social bond. Grooming also helps cats fend off stress. Veterinary experts report that a cat's heart rate actually slows down during a self-grooming session.

As for Chandler, it doesn't look like he has a future as a circus cat performing acrobatic stunts. When cats get caught doing something that startles or surprises them, they instinctively turn to grooming as a way to calm down, collect their thoughts, and restore dignity. It is as if they are saying, "What? I fell?

Surely you jest. Why, I'm just making myself look marvelous." Dogs, by contrast, take note of their favorite humans laughing when they do something silly and will try to replicate it to garner even more attention. They don't care about preserving their canine dignity.

Even though it is hard to resist laughing and pointing at Chandler, try to stifle your giggles. Instead, be his pal by calmly calling him over for a head scratch or a little treat. He will appreciate your gesture. 🐾

Strays Turned Stars

Sure, it's tricky to train dogs to perform the cha-cha onstage or to ace a top-level agility course in a national competition. So consider the guts—and skills—it takes to stake your livelihood on independent-minded cats performing before sold-out audiences. That's what renowned animal trainer Samantha Martin has been doing since 2005 as the chief executive human for the Amazing Acro-Cats.

As she can attest, nothing teaches you humility like a trained cat deciding whether or not to act in front of a live audience.

Martin and her Amazing Acro-Cats travel by tour bus all over North America. Martin has a knack for finding talent in rescued strays and shelter cats. Her troupe includes a groundhog named Garfield and a chicken named Cluck Norris.

This is young Rusty in his performing days. He still loves to do tricks and get treats!

Her go-to training tools are a target stick and a clicker, plus plenty of treats and positive-reinforcement praise. Clicker training involves "marking" a desired behavior like *Sit* or *Sit up* with pressing down on a metal clicker as soon as the behavior is done and then immediately handing over a treat. Eventually, the cat learns to pair that act with a specific phrase, such as *Good sit*. Targeting involves using a long stick with a round end to direct a cat to move from one place to another.

During the show, Martin's cats perform a variety of talents, from rising up on their hind legs and pushing a tiny shopping cart across the stage to weaving through agility poles to climbing a mini flagpole and unfurling the flag to ringing bells on cue. A handful of her four-legged feline talents play instruments, cat-style, as members of Tuna and the Rock-Cats.

In between shows, she fosters shelter cats and kittens at her place in Georgia, aptly named Meowy Manor. She has found homes for hundreds of cats. One of them is my ginger cat named Rusty the Purrformer. Martin found him as a flea-ridden orphan kitten and nursed him back to health. She also trained him to perform a variety of tricks. By 6 months of age, Rusty had the skills and desire to participate in the show. He would sit on a mark onstage and then leap through a hoop and land on another platform, earning treats and applause.

Because she had several ginger cats in her act, she asked me if I would make him part of my gang. Naturally, I said yes.

Although your cat may never step into the spotlight as a touring member of the Amazing Acro-Cats, you will both benefit when you invest the time to teach new tricks or behaviors. After all, cats who are mentally stimulated are less inclined to display behavior problems or to gain weight from inactivity. Who knows? A star may be born, even if the stage is only inside your home.

Thinking
OUTSIDE
the BOX

Feline bathroom habits— or the lack of them—are the top cat issue I've heard about during my more than two decades as a pet behaviorist. This is serious stuff for people, but it is literally life-or-death for far too many cats. The overriding behavioral reason people surrender their cats to animal shelters is because they can't deal with their cats' bathroom habits.

No one likes to come home and be bombarded by the stench of cat urine or discover a poop pile on the living room rug. People understandably become frustrated by accidents and tired of cleaning up messes. Sometimes a partner issues an ultimatum: Either persuade the cat to use the litter box or get rid of the cat.

There are many reasons why some cats bypass the litter box and go elsewhere. The cause may be a medical condition or stress-induced changes in the home routine or a dislike of the available "facilities." Either way, your cat is conveying that something is wrong. It is up to you to act like a pet detective and track down clues.

In this section, I share some scenarios with the hope that my answers enable you and your cat to enjoy many happy and incident-free years together in a home that always smells like a beautiful spring day. And maybe, just maybe, unwanted feline bathroom habits will no longer rule as the number one cat issue. Ready to make a positive change? Let's begin.

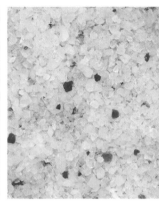

LITANY OF LITTER

Help! I am confused by all the types of litter available. There are so many different materials, and some are much pricier than others. Some are really heavy, but I wonder if the lightweight ones are as effective. And there's the whole scented versus unscented issue. What's the best type of litter to buy for my cats?

Litter options have been evolving much as coffee has. It used to be your choices in coffee were either black or with cream and sugar. Now, instead of ordering a plain cup of joe, you have to choose from espresso, latte, mocha, cold brew, or French press, among many other options.

Cat litter first hit store shelves shortly after World War II ended. Credit a clever young guy named Edward Lowe who worked in his dad's industrial absorbent company. One day, a friend complained to him about the smell and the mess of using dirt and ash in a box for her cat. Lowe suggested she sprinkle some of the company's absorbent material in the box to quell the hold-your-nose odor. Voilà! The birth of litter. Lowe launched Kitty Litter in 1947 and sold his company in 1990 for a whopping $200 million.

Today, the litter industry tops $2 billion in sales. Yes, that is with a B. The litter industry is highly competitive with companies trying to achieve brand loyalty from cat owners who live with more than 95 million pet cats in the United States alone.

For many years, the go-to choice was clay litter. Clay litter comes in clumping and nonclumping varieties and is generally inexpensive. But boxes of clay litter are heavy to lug from the store to your vehicle and into your house. Clay litter is also dusty, causing respiratory issues in some people and cats and leaving dusty paw tracks on floors.

In the past decade or so, companies have produced lightweight versions that weigh up to 50 percent less than regular clumping litter. They are also improving the packaging to make the product easier to pick up and pour. Packaging is often made from recycled materials.

Growing in popularity are litters made from unscented clumping crystals. These crystals do a good job of controlling odor and tend to last longer than clay types, but they cost more. One brand playfully offers crystal cat litter in eye-popping bright hues of green, pink, blue, and orange. Cats don't seem to care about the bright colors, but their people like the look. Crystals are soft on cat paws, lighter than most clay litters, and provide odor control.

Many companies are now making litter from wood, grain, and other products that absorb well and are biodegradable. Let's run through some of the more environmentally friendly litter materials.

- **Recycled newspaper.** Extra! Extra! Read all about it! This type of litter is giving a second life to discarded newspapers. The litter is soft, dust-free, and consists of tiny paper pellets. Most versions are nonclumping.

- **Wood.** Litters made of wood byproducts are very absorbent and control odors well. They come in the form of pellets, shavings, or a more crumbled version that is scoopable. Some cats don't mind the fresh scent of pine or fir, but others are not fans of these odors.

- **Grain.** Grains such as wheat and corn contain a natural enzyme that tones down the powerful ammonia odor in cat urine. Grain-based litters are touted as flushable, biodegradable, and not very dusty.

- **Other plants.** Litters made of bamboo, grass seed, tea leaves, and coconut husks may be a bit more expensive, but they are biodegradable, lightweight, and absorbent. There are different textures available, in both clumping and nonclumping versions. Most are not dusty, but some cats do have allergic reactions to some grasses or other plants, so if you try one of these, keep an eye on your cat for a few days.

117

Top Reasons That Cats Skip the Litter Box

In no particular order:

- Medical condition such as urinary tract infection
- Physical discomfort in entering and exiting litter box
- Dirty litter box
- Too few litter boxes for cats in the home
- Dislikes the texture of the litter
- New brand of litter used
- Household renovations or other disturbance
- Move to a new home
- New cat, dog, or person added to the household
- Change in owner's schedule
- Seeing an outdoor cat from inside and feeling threatened

To help you narrow your choices, keep in mind that a feline's nose is at least 100 times more sensitive than a person's nose. In addition, cats are not big fans of citrus or perfume smells. What your nose may detect as a light, welcoming hint of citrus can overpower a "scent-sitive" cat and might even evoke a litter box boycott. This also applies to deodorizing products that stick on walls or litter boxes. Nix that idea and use air-purifying machines next to the boxes instead.

Size also matters to most cats. Put yourself in your cat's paws for a moment. Would you rather walk on a fine-grained surface or a rocky road filled with large-size pellets? Your cat may be part of the feline majority and prefer the fine-grained clumping clay or could surprise you by liking the large pellet type.

In summary, put your cat's needs and desires first. Test her preferences by buying small bags of a couple of different types of litter. Put one in one litter box and the other in a second box and see which one your cat visits repeatedly.

One sure sign that your cat does not like the choice of litter is if he eliminates right next to the box. He is showing you that he is trying to do the right thing, but he doesn't want to come in contact with that type of litter. 🐾

LOCATION, LOCATION, LOCATION

We have a two-story home with three bedrooms and three bathrooms. We also have an enclosed patio. We have two indoor cats, ages 3 and 9. I want to put the litter box in the master bathroom where I can easily clean it, but my husband insists that it belongs in the basement. Where is the best place in the house to locate a litter box?

First of all, make that litter *boxes*. Veterinarians and animal behaviorists are united in this litter box math equation: Every household needs one litter box per cat plus one extra. In your case, that number totals three. Giving your cats choices increases the likelihood that they will routinely use a box instead of choosing a corner of the living room. If one cat stakes out a particular box, the other cat still has a place to go.

Another cardinal rule is to locate a litter box on each level of your home. You want to make litter boxes easily accessible to ensure that they will be used. As cats enter their senior years, they may develop arthritis, making it challenging to go up and down stairs. All cats of all ages need and deserve feline bathrooms that are convenient to reach on every floor.

As for where, think like a furry real estate agent for a moment. With cats, it is all about location, location, location when it comes to litter boxes. Cats like their litter boxes in quiet locales that provide them with privacy. In your home, that could mean in the master

bathroom as you suggest, plus a corner on the patio or in a den or bathroom. The basement or laundry room might work fine but be aware that some cats find these places to be dark and damp, or may be frightened when the washer and dryer are running. And remember

that the less conveniently located the litter boxes are, the less likely you are to regularly scoop them out.

Never place litter boxes near food and water bowls. It is a common misconception that this placement will serve as a reminder to cats to use the bathroom after meals. You are more likely to stir up a litter box boycott, because cats do not like to relieve themselves where they dine and drink.

Finally, position the litter boxes so they offer a welcoming entrance and escape route. This is important to prevent a cat using a litter box from being startled or tormented by a second cat or visiting dogs or guests. Be sure to escort your kitties to each new litter box location so they are aware of their bathroom options.

And one more tip: If you have dogs, especially those bent on sneaking a "snack" from a litter box, place a baby gate across the doorway to the room containing the litter box. I use a pet gate with vertical bars and a small opening at the bottom for my cats to easily slip through to access their litter boxes. This gate keeps my dog Kona from gaining access to any stinky "snacks" in the litter boxes. Vertical bars are better than horizontal ones that might serve to help a smart dog scramble up and over the gate. 🐾

Starting from Scratch

Very often, the reason a cat is not using a litter box is because of a medical or physical condition. A urinary tract or bladder infection, an injury, intestinal parasites—there are many causes. If a cat experiences pain while urinating or eliminating, he may associate the box itself with the pain and go elsewhere in an attempt to find a more comfortable spot.

Whenever a cat displays a change in elimination habits, the first thing the owner should do is make an appointment for a thorough exam to rule out any physical problems. Heed this advice: If you notice your cat crying out or straining while urinating, or producing only a few drops of urine, contact your veterinarian pronto. This is a life-threatening emergency because after just 24 hours of not urinating, a cat can die from urinary toxicity or kidney shutdown.

It is always better for your veterinarian to tell you "Everything is fine; it's just a minor issue that we can easily treat" than to have to ask, "Why did you wait so long?"

SCHOOLING KITTENS ON LITTER BOX PROTOCOLS

We're excited about adopting our first kitten. I thought kittens knew instinctively how to use a litter box from day one, but my cat friends say that isn't always the case. If the kitten we bring home needs help learning how to use the litter box, what's the best way to train her?

I bet you never imagined that someday you would add "litter box tutor" to your list of accomplishments. It may not be as impressive as brain surgeon or world's best mom, but for your young kitten, a little litter box guidance will go a long way in ensuring she practices a lifetime of good bathroom habits.

True, most kittens take to litter like, well, grown cats take to catnip. Generally, house cats instinctively bury their feces and cover up urine deposits, a behavior that dates back thousands of years to when wild cats needed to avoid detection by possible predators. That's why outdoor cats often choose the garden or sandbox for toileting, much to the dismay of gardeners and parents.

Most kittens learn the basic ABCs of litter box lessons from their mothers by about 4 weeks of age. It's a case of "kittens see, kittens do," in their quest to mimic Mom. Kittens who are orphaned or weaned away from their mothers at a very early age may be clueless about litter box etiquette. Or they may just be slow learners.

Here are some tips to help your new kitten ace her litter lesson.

- Purchase a small litter box with low sides (no higher than 3 inches) so your kitten can easily climb in and out. Boxes with sides 4 inches or higher or the kind with hoods can be intimidating.

- Locate the litter box in a place in your house that is easy to access but not in a noisy, high-traffic area like the kitchen. Never place the litter box near the food and water bowls. Cats are clean creatures and abhor the notion of having their chow next to their bathroom. If you live in a multilevel house, locate a litter box on each level.

- When you bring home your new kitten, escort her to the litter box (filled with about 2 inches of litter) and place her in the box. Gently move her front paws through the litter to let her feel the texture. Use your index finger to paw through the clean litter. Then let her explore the litter box and jump out on her own.

- During the first few days after her arrival, place her in the litter box when she first wakes up, after she eats, after a play session, and after she wakes from a catnap.

- After placing her in the litter box, quietly step back and leave her be. Unlike puppies who love to hear an owner sing out *Good potty!* in a happy voice, most felines prefer privacy and don't wish for you to bring out the band or applaud when they accomplish their mission. Be more subdued with your kitten.

- Be sure to scoop out the deposits daily to keep the litter box clean. This needs to be a lifelong habit to keep your house smelling great and to encourage your cat to pick the litter box as her bathroom for her entire lifetime.

- Practice the two Ps of potty training: patience and punishment-free. Your youngster may need just a few trips to the litter box to get the hang of things, or it might take her several weeks. Resist the temptation to scold or yell or squirt her with a water bottle, because the punishment approach usually backfires. Your kitten may become so frightened that she starts to avoid the litter box and hunts for less scary places like under your bed or in your closet.

If you notice any signs of diarrhea or straining or your kitten cries when using the litter box, please take her to your veterinarian to be examined for a possible medical problem such as urinary tract disease or intestinal parasites. Good luck! 🐾

DECODING WEIRD LITTER BOX ACTIONS

I've had cats all my life. Most were champs at using their litter boxes. But a few of them display some strange behaviors, such as the desire to sleep in a just-scooped litter box or not covering their poop. One of my cats, Joey, makes me laugh when he rolls happily in the litter box and then dashes out with a look of glee. What's happening?

Who said cats don't have a sense of humor? Especially bathroom humor. Let me run down some examples of odd potty habits in cats from perplexed people. Let's start with sleeping or playing in a just-scooped litter box. The size of the litter box appeals to some cats seeking cozy spots for naps, and the play is activated usually by kittens or juveniles who feel safe in the litter box and need a way to expel pent-up energy. Of course, that means a litter mess for you to clean up.

Now, let's address baffling deposit habits. Some cats choose to poop in one litter box and urinate in a second one. The reason remains a feline mystery but be grateful that your picky cat is using litter boxes and not your floor. Cats who do their deeds and walk out without covering their poop do so on purpose. It tends to be a habit from confident cats to communicate to other cats in the home. Uncovered poop emits a strong scent as a signal to other cats that this cat feels he is the boss of the house. It's like potty graffiti to declare, "A cool cat was here."

Some cats will rub their faces and paws all over the sides of a new litter box—or a just-cleaned litter box containing fresh litter. Cats have scent glands in their cheeks and paws and the rubbing releases these glands to tell other pets in the house that they are claiming this new litter box or new litter. 🐾

PUTTING A LID ON IT—NOT!

We have two neutered males, ages 2 and 3. Both are good about using the open-style litter boxes we have for them in a couple of different rooms. We are thinking about renovating our home and I may want to switch to litter boxes with hoods or ones tucked into furniture to hide them from view of our guests. Any suggestions for transitioning them to hooded litter boxes?

The go-to litter box for decades has been the classic shallow open box, but we live in an era of home improvement, and the desire to renovate and decorate extends to our feline bathrooms. Litter box options offer covered styles, self-cleaning boxes, round or oval models, and ones that tuck nicely into corners. There are even litter boxes that slip inside end tables or other pieces of furniture that keep the feline facilities out of sight.

Because your two cats have used the open-style boxes with no issues, I would recommend that you keep your old ones for now and introduce a third with a hood as a test model in a different room. Some cats feel more

secure using a litter box with a hood because it provides them with more privacy. Hooded types keep more litter in boxes especially when used by cats who like to kick up a fuss while burying their deposits. Covered boxes also make it harder for household dogs to conduct litter box raids.

However, I am not a fan of hooded boxes or concealed-in-furniture litter boxes for several reasons. For starters, hooded boxes harbor odor—a huge turnoff—and may trigger a boycott in some cats whose sense of smell puts ours to shame.

You must be vigilant and scoop them daily and clean them using warm

124

water and mild detergent at least once a month and allow time for them to dry completely. Hooded litter boxes can create a case of "out of sight, out of mind" in some pet parents. Professional pet sitters tell me of their frustration in dealing with neglected boxes that are overfilled with urine clumps and poop deposits.

Another issue is that hooded types may feel a bit cramped for larger or longer-bodied cats to get into position and squat without bumping into the sides or hitting their heads. Finally, hooded litter boxes and ones tucked into end tables may win decor points, but they only offer one opening. This may not be a problem for a single cat, but in this case, if one cat is using it and the second cat decides to stalk and pounce, the first cat is a sitting target. It could trigger some behavior issues between your cats and even spark a feline fight.

For years, I was a daily newspaper reporter always trying to get a scoop on the competition. But these days, my scooping is more headline-worthy because I am ensuring that my cats can rely on clean bathrooms every day. So my vote is to stick with open litter boxes and to place them in various rooms for your cats. You can disguise them with foldable privacy screens, but make sure there are multiple points of access.

NEW HOUSE, NEW PROBLEM

I have a 3-year-old, neutered, domestic shorthair named Winston. My husband and I recently moved from a two-bedroom condo to a four-bedroom detached house. I noticed no urine in the litter pan, so I started looking and found that Winston had urinated on an unpacked box in a spare room.

We moved a mattress down to the basement so we could have something to sit on until we get a couch, and Winston urinated on that as well. The problem is, we are ordering a new couch. How can we make sure he doesn't urinate on that as well?

Cats behave like feline Zorros. They like to leave their mark on their home turf. Most of the time, they do this by rubbing scent glands from their feet, cheeks, face, and tail on various places inside the home. But sometimes they mark with urine to proclaim ownership or to communicate to other cats within the household or to those lurking outside the back door.

Indoor cats protect their territory just as carefully as outdoor ones. Home represents a place of safety and comfort. Cats also crave routine and abhor change. It is not unusual for a cat in a new home to react by "forgetting" his previous toileting habits. Winston is doing what comes naturally to a nervous cat—he is marking his new territory with his scent as a way to feel more at home. The items you mentioned contain familiar smells from your condo that Winston misses, and to boost his confidence, he may feel the need to reinforce his markings on them.

Veterinary studies identify several common causes behind urine marking: interactions with other cats outside the home, interactions with cats inside the home, limited access to the outdoors,

relocation to a new home, and changes in an owner's daily schedule.

Although cats of either gender will urine mark, intact males are most likely to do so. They use their strong and pungent urine as a way to attract females in the surrounding area. Fortunately, your cat has been neutered, which tones down the odor.

Please rule out any possible medical condition that may be responsible for Winston's changes in bathroom habits. If none are found, then the next strategy is to make your new home more welcoming to Winston.

Start by providing new litter boxes and fresh litter. Clean the litter boxes daily. Limit Winston's access to various parts of the new house when you are not at home and definitely make the basement off-limits. Do not yell at or hit Winston. You will only elevate his stress and probably prompt him to perform more marking. As he becomes comfortable in his new territory, you can gradually increase his access to the rest of the house.

Urine contains pheromones that communicate a cat's health and mood. There is a product called Feliway that has been demonstrated to be effective in curbing behavior-related urine marking. Feliway is a chemical version of the feline facial pheromone. It works because cats tend not to urine mark locations where they have already left their facial pheromones.

This product comes in a spray as well as a diffuser that plugs into an electric outlet. The diffuser emits this synthetic scent (humans can't smell it) 24 hours a day and lasts for about one month. You can spray Feliway directly onto urine marks and household items such as sofas, drapes, and doorframes without worrying that it will cause a stain.

In extreme cases, urine-marking cats may need calming medications for a period of time. Studies have shown that these drugs can reduce incidents of urine marking up to 75 percent. I urge you to work closely with your veterinarian in administering these medications and then gradually wean your cat off them.

We are fortunate that we have many more weapons available today than a decade ago to counter urine marking, but it still requires patience, consistency, and compliance on the part of owners to ensure success. 🐾

Is It Spraying or Marking?

When describing cats who urinate outside their litter boxes, people often aren't sure if the cat is spraying or marking. In fact, the terms can be used interchangeably. The only difference is body position and, sometimes, the volume of urine that is released.

Spraying occurs when a cat backs up against a vertical surface, such as a wall, and squirts urine while standing. In essence, the cat is leaving "pee-mails." Both male and female cats will spray, although the behavior is far more common in males, particularly unneutered ones. Intact males spray as a form of sexual advertising and as a threat to other males.

Marking happens when a cat squats and urinates on a horizontal surface, such as a bed. A cat who is upset with his owner for some reason (working late hours or adopting a kitten) may urinate on objects that the cat clearly associates with the owner such as a bed, sofa, or briefcase. This behavior is triggered by emotional stress or general apprehension (from watching their beloved owner pack a suitcase, for example).

Both spraying and marking should be distinguished as behavioral issues. However, keep in mind that some cats avoid the litter box simply because they don't like the location (perhaps it's near a noisy washing machine), detest the type of litter (especially citrus scented), or are unable to perform in the litter box due to a health problem.

MY CAT PEES ON MY BED

I jokingly refer to Benny, my 3-year-old neutered cat, as Velcro because he follows me from room to room when I am home. He also sleeps on my bed each night, often settling down there before I do. Everything was fine until I adopted a small puppy named Gracie, who is very sweet. Benny hisses at her and doesn't like it when Gracie tries to sleep on the bed at night. On a few occasions, Benny has peed on the bed. What can I do to get Benny to accept Gracie?

Some high-strung cats or solo felines in a home become very attached to their owners. To embellish a Shakespearean quote, "Beware of feline jealousy—it is the green-eyed monster." Benny is not about to let a mere mutt muscle in and challenge him as top cat of the household. Because your Pee Prince can't engage in a conversation with Gracie, he tells her in the best way he knows, by marking the disputed territory with his urine.

My advice is to give Gracie her own bed in your bedroom. Motivate her to settle down there by leaving treats on her bed at night. Think of it as a canine version of the mints left on pillows in fancy hotel rooms. You may need to reinforce her new sleeping arrangement by calmly saying *Off* if she jumps on your bed. Usher her back to her own bed and reward her for lying down on it. Gracie should be content with being in the same room as you and her feline mate, Benny.

Reinforce Benny's rank by greeting him first when you come home and feeding him ahead of Gracie. Benny definitely will be paying attention to all of this and will note that Gracie ranks number three in the household. Time is your ally. As Benny sees that this cute pup isn't leaving, but that he still reigns as "top dog" at bedtime and mealtimes, he will become more confident and not need to mark.

I also advise you to keep the bedroom door closed while you're gone and until you go to bed to limit Benny's access. To oust his urine odor from your bedding, clean thoroughly with a protein enzymatic cleaner available at hardware or pet supply stores or from your veterinarian. 🐾

Identifying the Culprit

If you share your home with two or more cats and one is boycotting the litter box, how do you identify the culprit? Don't look for the guilty feline to step forward and confess.

Here is a colorful solution if your perpetrator is pooping outside the box:

Select the most likely cat and give him a few drops of red or green food coloring by mouth or in some canned food. His stool will look distinctly more vibrant than those produced by the other cats. If the stool outside the box looks normal, you know the other cat is the problem. (If you have more than one cat, wait a few days and test another cat or give two cats different colors, which is a bit more efficient!)

If the issue is urination outside the litter box, contact your veterinarian about providing you with an ophthalmic dye called fluorescein that you give orally. Don't worry, it will not harm your cat. At night, you shine a black light around your home for urine spots, which appear as a bright fluorescent tone.

Once you have identified which cat is missing the box, book an appointment with your veterinarian to rule out any possible medical causes for his litter box avoidance before resorting to behavioral tactics described in this section.

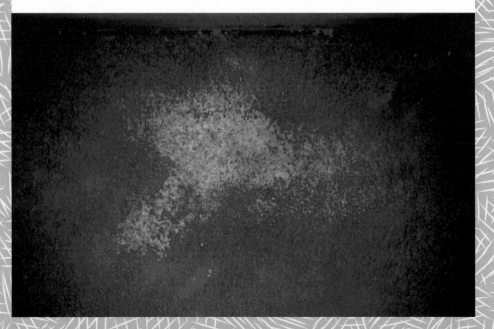

STYMIED BY STOOL SITUATION

We adopted a healthy 12-week-old kitten. At first, we kept him in the bathroom at night and when we were not at home. I put a covered litter box in the bathroom with his food and water and bedding and a toy. He peed in the litter box but pooped in the bathtub. Now that he is older, he has full run of the house. We keep the litter box clean, scooping it every day, but he poops on the tile floor next to the litter box. I am tired of cleaning it up. What can I do to get him to use the litter box?

The one saving grace is that your young cat is targeting easy-to-clean flooring surfaces rather than carpets or furniture. Having become accustomed to using the smooth tub, he is continuing to find a familiar surface. Your young but savvy feline is trying to tell you that he is not jazzed by the litter box shape, size, or location, or by the type of litter.

Too often, people forget that litter box usage needs to be addressed from the cat's point of view, not theirs. Keep in mind that urinating takes less time than defecating. Your kitten may not like to spend a lot of time in the litter box and so may opt to defecate outside the litter box where he can survey his surroundings and feel a bit safer.

Perhaps the litter box is too small or too large or too deep for his liking. I recommend that you add a second litter box of a different size without a hood. Position this one near the "scene of the crime" but initially do not put in any litter. Instead, leave it empty to create a smooth surface to attract your kitten.

You may discover that he appreciates this new feline bathroom customized to his liking. At first, you can reach for some toilet paper to scoop up the deposits and flush them. Once he's using the empty box regularly, you can begin slowly adding litter, just a handful or two at a time, until he's used to the feel of it.

Also, make sure his bathroom is out of sight from his favorite catnap spot and his water and food bowls. Cats prefer to have these feline necessities spaced apart.

As with all elimination problems, you should have your veterinarian give your kitten a head-to-tail examination to verify that no medical problem exists. Some intact males will do fecal marking, so if you have not done so already, book an appointment to have your kitten neutered. That often cuts down on inappropriate elimination behavioral issues and also reduces his risk for developing prostate cancer.

WHAT'S THE SCOOP ON CAT POOP?

My veterinarian always wants me to bring in a fecal sample when I bring in Barry, my 8-year-old longhaired cat, for his annual physical exam. Why is that necessary? Having to scoop up poop in a plastic bag and transport it in my car makes me cringe a bit. What can a veterinarian learn from analyzing feline poop?

Yes, one of the less glamorous aspects of being a pet parent is the daily must-do of scooping litter boxes of urine clumps and poop droppings. But here's the deal: Poop happens. The way it looks and smells provides veterinarians with a wealth of information about the health condition of pets and may be a vital clue to the onset of a condition that could be successfully treated early before it erupts into a major, and more expensive, health issue.

If Barry's poop looks odd, smells foul, occurs too often or too little, is red (possibly blood) or pale yellow (possibly issues with the pancreas or liver), pay heed.

These are clues that something is wrong with the pet's diet or there's a medical condition brewing, such as constipation, inflammatory bowel disease, or even colon cancer.

In my pet first aid/CPR classes, I playfully alert my students to the need to become poopologists. For starters, I identify the four Cs of pet poop.

Consistency. The deposits from the pet should be segmented, the consistency of modeling clay, and easy to pick up.

Color. Color should be chocolate brown. Bright red may indicate bleeding in the lower gastrointestinal tract. Maroon-colored stools could indicate bleeding in the stomach or small intestines. Pale yellow deposits may signal something is wrong with the liver, pancreas, or gallbladder.

Contents. Hold your nose and inspect the poop. Report any signs of rice-shaped flecks or wriggly strands that could signal the cat has worms. Too much hair in the stool can be attributed to overgrooming due to stress, allergies, or a host of medical conditions.

Coating. Gross as it sounds, when you scoop the poop off the floor or from the litter box, it should not leave any residue or filmy mucus.

When it comes to producing healthy poop, veterinarians have been keeping a not-so-hidden secret. They actually rank the poop brought into their clinics on a scale of 1 to 7. The healthiest poop earns a rating between 2 and 3.

Here is the rundown on the fecal scoring system used by veterinarians to rate kitty poo.

1. Hard, small pellets resembling Milk Duds; could indicate dehydration

2. Tootsie-roll in color and texture; segmented

3. Ideal: Chocolate brown–colored logs easy to pick up and slightly squishable

4. Chocolate, gray, or tan-colored logs with a slimy coating

5. Moist, slimy logs that fall apart when picked up and leave a residue

6. Shapeless plops of poop often dropped in multiple locations

7. Watery, reddish brown, or tan-colored diarrhea; can cause dehydration

And that's the scoop on cat poop! So the next time you are transporting Barry and his poo to the veterinary clinic, congratulate yourself on being a responsible pet parent. 🐾

YOWLING IN THE LITTER BOX

My cat, Cowboy, never misses the litter box. I can count on him producing two or three urine clumps and one or two poop deposits each day. He just celebrated his seventh birthday and now I have noticed that Cowboy is making frequent trips to the litter box but producing only small amounts of urine. Sometimes he will squat and nothing comes out, but he gives a little cry as if he is in pain. What is happening?

When a cat who has good bathroom habits starts to show distress in the litter box, the cause is generally medical, not behavioral. Please have Cowboy checked pronto by your veterinarian.

A few years ago, I noticed that my cat Casey stood in the litter box for a long time, then moaned as he squatted briefly before springing out. I inspected to find a tiny circle of urine with blood. I knew this was a medical emergency. I placed Casey in his travel carrier,

gathered the urine sample in a bag, and took him to a 24-hour animal emergency center. The veterinarians were able to quickly unblock his urethra but they kept him overnight to monitor him and to perform further tests. I will never forget the veterinarian saying to me: "I am so glad you brought Casey in immediately. If you had waited until the morning, he might have died."

All cats can be at risk for urinary stones or crystals, blockages, infections, and a host of other issues. Plumbing problems in cats, especially male cats, come in many forms and can strike quickly. When a cat has a urinary obstruction, it is a true medical emergency. When a cat can't urinate, toxins build up in the blood and the condition can cause life-threatening organ failure, including to the heart.

Heed these signs that you need to take your cat to the veterinary clinic pronto:

- Crying while urinating
- Excessive grooming of the genitals
- Bypassing the litter box to urinate elsewhere
- Having difficulty urinating
- Seeing blood in your cat's urine

Any and all of these signs can indicate a blockage in the urethra, the development of urinary or bladder stones, stress-induced urinary tract infection, bladder wall inflammation, or a host of conditions that fall under the blanket term known as feline lower urinary tract disease (FLUTD). Your veterinarian will perform a thorough exam that often includes taking blood and urine samples and performing an ultrasound to look for evidence of stones or crystals. Your veterinarian may prescribe medications to relax muscles, reduce stress, or fight infections in your cat; in some cases, surgery may be required.

Your veterinarian may also recommend adding key supplements to your cat's diet. Popular go-to choices include zylkene and cosequin. Zylkene is a stress-reducing supplement made from casein, a milk protein with calming properties. Cosequin is a natural supplement used to help cats with bladder and joint issues. It comes as a capsule that can be sprinkled on a cat's food or as a chewable treat.

While you cannot prevent all plumbing issues, you can play a vital role in your cat's health and survival. That starts by paying attention to Cowboy's bathroom habits—which you are doing. Know what is normal for your cat in terms of frequency and size of the deposits in the litter box. And strive to increase your cat's water consumption to prevent dehydration that can exacerbate urinary issues. Here's wishing a long, healthy life for Cowboy and my Casey. 🐾

feline fact

Crème Puff reigns as the Methuselah of felines. This cat died in 2005 at the grand old age of 38.

Novel Cat Bathroom Options

If your cat is not using the litter box and medical issues have been ruled out, he may be seeking novel surfaces to urinate on. Dusty Rainbolt is a cat behavior consultant and expert on all things cat p-e-e. To keep your cat in your home and not surrendered to a shelter, consider these creative options from Dusty.

- Use large plastic storage bins with low, easy-to-access sides for litter boxes.

- Potty training mats for puppies absorb a lot of urine. Some are machine washable.

- Cat diapers will keep pee off walls and rugs, but you need to monitor closely and replace regularly several times a day. You don't want your cat to incur ammonia burns on his bum from a wet or dirty cat diaper left on too long.

SHOULD MY CAT USE MY TOILET?

I love my cat, Beyonce, but not her litter box. I hate the smell and the mess, and I hate dealing with the litter. I live in a tiny apartment with a bath-and-a-half, so I have two toilets. A few days a week, I work from home. I don't want to scoop the litter box every day or clean it every week. I am thinking about trying to get her to use my spare toilet and ditching the litter box. Any advice?

Don't make the switch. Veterinarians and feline behaviorists identify so many negatives associated with trying to get a cat to use a toilet. I know scooping litter clumps is not a fun task, but it takes me a whopping 5 minutes every day to scoop five litter boxes for my four cats.

I use a Litter Genie (the feline equivalent of a diaper pail). Clumps go into a bag in a covered container that eliminates odor, and I discard the bag once a week.

Here are a few more reasons not to toilet train your cat.

- A guest shuts the door or puts down the lid, blocking Beyonce's access.

- In a rare moment of feline clumsiness, Beyonce falls into the bowl, giving her a very negative association with using the toilet. She may look for other places to relieve herself.

- If Beyonce has to stay overnight at the veterinarian or a pet-boarding facility, she'll have to use a litter box, not a toilet.

I could go on, but for Beyonce's mental well-being and to prevent her from feeling the need to relieve herself on your rug, pillow, or other inappropriate place, please step up your litter box duties. It's a quick, easy way to show Beyonce how much you care for her. 🐾

LITTER BOX ATTACKS

I have a sweet, shy cat named Princess and a bold one named Max. I adopted Princess first, about two years before bringing Max home as a kitten from my local animal shelter. Princess is now 3 and Max is 1. They get along fine until Princess tries to use the litter box. The litter box is located in the corner of a closet in the spare bedroom. Max seems to enjoy stalking her and pouncing on her when she tries to go.

I yell at Max, but it doesn't stop him. Poor Princess is becoming a bundle of nerves. She hasn't made any messes outside the litter box, but I'm afraid she may start. Any answers?

Kittens will be kittens, but this is not acceptable. In a multi-cat situation, a dominant cat will pick on a shy cat. Princess's nature is to be nonconfrontational, while Max is clearly more outgoing. Max is also younger and more rambunctious, while Princess has left her silly kitten days behind her.

With the one and only litter box located in a corner of a closet, Princess has no way to flee the scene when attacked. She feels trapped, and you are right to worry that in time she may start secretly urinating behind the couch and other places.

The first thing you need to do is add two more litter boxes. The recommended number is one per cat plus one extra. Max cannot guard three litter boxes at one time. With more spots to choose from, he may feel less inclined to protect "his" litter box.

Place the new litter boxes in different rooms. Position them away from walls and in more open areas so Princess can view the room or see the doorway. This will give her a little more time to see Max coming and be better prepared.

Tempting as it is, do not yell at Max. You will only escalate the tension and anxiety that both animals are feeling. Instead, distract Max when you see Princess head to a litter box by engaging him in play or bribing him with a treat. Finally, if you have not already neutered Max, please do so. That will also tone down his bullying tendencies. 🐾

137

Ousting Odors and Stomping Stains

Unfortunately, many household cleaners only temporarily mask the pungent smell of urine, vomit, or feces that stubbornly fester in carpet fibers or hardwood floors. But your home need not smell like the local zoo. The sweet smell of success requires a basic understanding of the chemical makeup of urine, feces, and vomit.

Composed of organic amines, sulfur, ammonia, and mercaptans, these carbon- and nitrogen-rich compounds attract naturally occurring bacteria in the home. The pungent odors that seem to worsen after using certain household cleaners are the result of volatile byproducts created by normal bacterial processes.

Attacking pet messes with household cleaners or homemade solutions containing ammonia or bleach can worsen the whiff and solidify the stain. Ammonia and bleach effectively kill germs, but they can cause respiratory issues, dizziness, vomiting, and damage to mucous membranes in

cats. Because cat urine contains ammonia, using ammonia to clean cat pee is basically communicating that it's okay to pee in that spot. Fortunately, there are more environmentally and pet-friendly cleaning products available. Consider these pet-safe options for cleaning: Better Life, Biokleen, and Seventh Generation.

(A safety note: When you are cleaning counters and floors with products containing ammonia or bleach, usher your cat into a comfy room with feline amenities and shut the door. Wait to let your cat into the rest of the house after the cleaned surfaces have dried completely. You don't want your cat getting these products on his fur, then ingesting them while grooming himself.)

Another common mistake is attacking soiled carpeting with a steam cleaner. Steam cleaners work great to remove ordinary dirt, but the heat bakes organic stains into the carpet fibers, leaving a permanent odor. Here are some tips for dealing with pet stains and smells.

Timing is key. The faster you can remove fresh urine, vomit, and feces, the fewer odors will be left behind. Poop is fairly easy to scoop with paper towels or a plastic bag, but urine stains are more challenging.

Soak it up. Remove as much urine as possible by blotting it up with paper towels, newspapers, or old cotton rags.

Keep pressing on these materials until you no longer see any yellow moisture. Don't rub! Rubbing pushes the urine deeper into the carpet.

Neutralize the odor. Apply a pet-stain enzymatic cleaner to the site. Follow label directions and allow the solution to set before soaking it up with paper or cotton towels. Be patient. Enzymatic products need at least 24 hours to successfully clean the area. Two highly effective enzymatic cleaners are Nature's Miracle and Zero Odor.

Bring on the baking soda. For urine-soaked bedding and other machine-washable materials, add one pound of baking soda (bicarbonate of soda) along with your detergent and wash with cold water. Baking soda naturally absorbs odors and discourages bacterial growth. Avoid hot water because heat can set the odor in the fabric.

Spotting old stains. Old pet messes, especially urine, may be difficult to locate. If you can't pinpoint a particular spot by sniffing it out, buy a black-light bulb that fits into a flashlight. At night, turn off the lights and survey surfaces with the black light to locate the greenish yellow fluorescent glow given off by old pet stains. Use chalk or other easy-to-clean materials to outline the stain to ensure complete cleanup. (See also Identifying the Culprit, page 129.)

The Basics of
CHOWING and
GROOMING

You probably know that cats are obligate carnivores, a fancy term that means they are meat eaters. The challenge comes in selecting the right ingredients in the right amounts and in the right form so they become the nutrients that keep a cat's body a-humming for a lifetime.

I had two choices when feeding my childhood cat, Corky: kibble or canned food. Feline dining options have greatly expanded, with the US pet food industry earning nearly $100 billion annually. The menu includes organic options, plant-based proteins, novel ingredients such as rabbit and bison, and frozen or freeze-dried versions. Also showing up in cat food and treats are trendy additives such as coconut, dandelion root, and honey. Supplements such as omega-3 fatty acids, prebiotics, probiotics, and even CBD oils are also being added to feline diets.

As much as cats love to eat, they were also born to groom. We're quite familiar with the saying, "Eeew. He smells like a dog." But I bet you have never heard someone declare in disgust: "Phew! He smells like a cat!" Cats can spend up to one-third of their waking hours fussing over their coats. When was the last time you spent that amount of time styling your hair?

In this section, I share some insights about two favorite feline pastimes: consuming and grooming. Read on!

FINICKY FEEDER

My cats have always been easy-to-please eaters. Not anymore. I recently brought in a stray cat, whom I'm guessing is about 3 years old. I thought she would be grateful to have a home, but she is quite picky about what she eats. My other two cats eat their dry food without any problem. This new cat, Gabby, does love salmon and tuna, but I can't keep catering to her expensive tastes.

While cats have long had a reputation as picky eaters, I prefer to regard them as discriminating. You need to assess what's going on. Is Gabby really being a picky eater or is something else at play? Write down Gabby's eating habits over the next few days. There are several possible explanations why she doesn't gobble her kibble.

Although she came to you as a stray, she may have been used to a different type of food if she had a previous home. Or she may be satisfied with treats and table scraps such as those pieces of delicious salmon and tuna you hand out.

Are the other cats blocking her from her bowl? Try setting out another one to lessen the competition. Speaking of bowls, some cats don't like their whiskers touching the sides and will walk away from their kibble if the bowl doesn't "fit." Gabby may need a larger or shallower bowl.

The location may also be a turnoff, especially if the food bowl is in a noisy, high-traffic area like the kitchen. Some cats like to dine without a lot of hoopla around them.

Does Gabby spend any time outside? She may have charmed a neighbor into giving her tasty treats or she may be filling up on mice and sparrows.

Finally, do not rule out a possible medical condition. Gabby may have tender gums or missing teeth that make chewing a challenge.

Cats like routines. If you feed your cats a variety of commercial dry food, Gabby may be holding out in hopes of something tastier than the current kibble. It's better to stick with one brand consistently. You may spice it up a bit by pouring a little sodium-free broth over the kibble, but once you find a good-quality cat food Gabby seems to like, stay with it. If her health needs change, switch her gradually to another type of food. I recommend working closely with your veterinarian on the best dietary choice. Good luck! 🐾

Lack of a Sweet Tooth

Open a can of tuna and watch your cat come running to share your lunch, but bring out a candy bar or a bag of cookies and he is most likely completely indifferent. Most cats are not interested in sweet treats.

All mammals have receptor cells located on their tongues that transmit taste signals to their brains. These receptor cells are clustered together as taste buds. Human receptor cells are capable of detecting five major taste sensations: salty, sweet, sour, bitter, and umami, which is a meaty or savory flavor found in fermented soy products, among other foods.

In terms of taste buds, people have about 9,000 compared to just 473 in cats. Cats are capable of detecting sour, salt, and bitter, but recent studies confirm that cats are the only mammals known to lack sweet receptors. Cats are at the very least, indifferent to sugar and at best, unable to detect it.

So why do some cats beg for a taste of ice cream or yogurt? These dairy products contain a large amount of a protein called casein, which is made of amino acids that cats need in their diets. Dairy products also tend to contain fat, and

cats are well suited to digesting and utilizing fats, although the lactose in milk isn't easily digested by felines.

But taste isn't everything. Because feline taste buds are few in number and poorly developed, cats depend more on their sense of smell than taste. They do not adopt the canine motto of "eat first, ask later" when it comes to food.

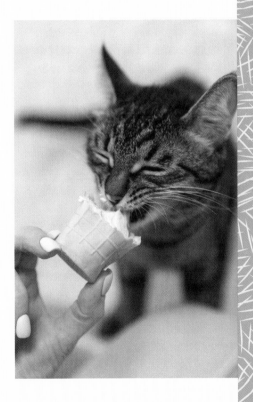

MEALTIME MAYHEM

I adore Sassy, my spirited young cat, except at mealtime. He transforms into a pushy, demanding bully who intimidates my other two cats away from their food bowls. He even tries to paw out kibble from my two dogs' bowls. Mealtime has become stressful, and it seems to be taking a toll on all of us. What can I do to make meals calmer and easier?

Feeding cats is more than simply filling the food bowl; it should be considered part of their environment enrichment. Being bullied or stressed at mealtimes can cause some cats to hide, lose their appetites, gorge their food quickly, drool, eliminate outside the litter boxes, claw sofas, fight with other pets in the home, and overgroom to the point of creating red, bald spots on their coats.

Medically, mealtime stress can trigger such conditions as urinary tract infections, feline idiopathic cystitis, weakened immune systems, and skin disease.

Sassy sounds like a copycat of my young cat, Rusty, who was rescued from a dumpster as an orphan kitten and knew what hungry felt like. During his first couple of weeks with us, his mealtime antics caused my other cats, Mikey and Casey, to gobble their food quickly before Rusty could finish his meal and try to take over their bowls. They started vomiting more and having runny stools and even occasionally refused to eat. Fortunately, my dogs respect cats

and would let Rusty elbow his way into their bowls.

To achieve calmness at mealtimes, I changed our entire routine. I now prepare all of their food bowls in the laundry room next to the kitchen with the door closed. I bring out Rusty's bowl first. He excitedly follows me into the hallway bathroom where I place his bowl and close the door. Next, I place food bowls for Casey and Mikey on the top shelves of the two cat trees in the living room with them looking in opposite directions. I feed my two larger dogs, Bujeau and Kona, on the floor at either end of the kitchen island that serves as a visual barrier. I place little dog Emma's bowl in a corner away from the island. After they all finish their meals at their own paces (and in peace), I pick up and clean their bowls before letting Rusty out.

I am happy to report the Rusty loves his solo dining experience. Try feeding Sassy by himself in a closed room, and I bet the rest of your pets will breathe a collective sigh of relief while they calmly eat at their own pace uninterrupted. 🐾

CHEW ON THIS

When I head out the door to go to work, I always give my dog a Kong toy stuffed with peanut butter. It seems to keep him occupied and happy for the entire day. I tried giving my cat, Garfield (yes, he's big and orange!), a small stuffed Kong toy. He just sniffed it and ignored it. Why isn't he attracted to Kong toys like Buddy is?

Cats and dogs have different jaw structures. They eat and chew differently. Cats are strict carnivores, whereas dogs are more omnivorous and eat a wider variety of foods. Cats' mouths feature sharp, slicing teeth that are designed to snare, hold, and tear apart small prey such as mice and birds. They use their barbed tongues to rasp away bits of meat, rather than relying primarily on their teeth. Feline jaws move up and down, while canine jaws are designed to crush bones and to grind back and forth.

Both dogs and cats have oral fixations. Dogs often pass time and calm themselves down by gnawing on bones. It helps them to relax. Cats often turn to grooming themselves when they feel stressed or unsettled. They like the contact of their barbed tongues on their fur. Grooming is their comfort activity of choice, not gnawing.

In general, cats are fussier about what they stick in their mouths than their kooky canine chums are. That explains why it is easier to fool a dog by hiding his pill in a piece of cheese than it is to fool a cat. Most dogs will gulp down the cheesy treat without hesitation, but most cats will sniff out that disgusting pill and either surgically nibble all the cheese off the pill or saunter out of the room without another glance.

Garfield would probably prefer food-dispensing toys and food puzzles to occupy his mind and to bring out his inner hunter during the day. Food puzzles and mini meals and even hiding food in a room for a cat to sniff out and find allow indoor cats to indulge the feline desire to hunt and catch multiple small meals a day, just like their big cousins in the wild. 🐾

DETERMINED CAT BURGLAR

My cat, Sophie, begs like a dog at dinnertime—only worse. At least with my dog, Joey, I can tell him to *Sit and leave it* or *Find your spot*. But not Sophie. She has no qualms or hesitations about jumping on the kitchen counter when I am cooking or trying to paw food from my plate when I am eating dinner. Mealtime has become a battle of wills. What can I do to enjoy my food and to stop her food-begging ways?

Dogs don't have a monopoly on being food beggars, but cats are far more mobile and usually more coy. They look at you with their adorable eyes and wink or softly tap your shin with a beseeching paw as you prepare to take a forkful of food. Or they deftly land in your lap and begin purring sweetly. You succumb and hand your cat a food morsel from your plate.

There are two reasons to discourage begging at your table. The first is your peace of mind and the second is your cat's health. If you are having trouble saying no to furry beggars, remind yourself that table scraps are often high in calories and low in nutritional value, especially if you allow Sophie to lap up gravy or to devour the fat from a piece of sirloin. Consuming the wrong food can cause vomiting, diarrhea, obesity, and a host of other health woes.

Healthy treats designed for cats are much better alternatives for snacking between meals, and you can use these food "bribes" to your advantage to reinforce good behavior. However, don't go hog wild on healthy treats either—limit them to about 10 percent of your cat's daily chow.

It sounds like Sophie has elected to step up her food-seeking game. Some cats develop their chowhound skills to the point that they reach PhD status (Panhandling for Dinner). I know. My otherwise sweet ginger boy, Casey, used to unleash his feline charm if I sat on the sofa with a plate containing chicken or cheese or, strangely, Cheetos. Like Sophie, he started with a loud purr and a gentle front paw tap to my wrist to remind me that sharing is a good trait.

I admit I did give him bits of my food at first. But I quickly paid the price. He stepped up his mooching game and began boldly trying to swipe food from my plate and dash off with it.

To put the brakes on begging, implement a new policy of feeding both your pets only from their food bowls. Yelling or pushing Sofie away won't work and may actually increase her attention-seeking determination. Instead, while you are cooking or eating, calmly usher Sophie into a room with a door you can close. Let her out after the table is cleared. Sanity will be restored.

Be patient. It will take some time and persistence to introduce this new routine and to stop Sophie from pestering you when human food is around. Naturally, the best advice is not to develop the habit of feeding your cat table scraps in the first place. That way, she will never know what she is missing. And you will ensure that she is more likely to stay at a healthy weight. 🐾

No-No People Foods for Cats

Here's a rundown of food safe for people that should never be dished up to cats.

- Raw fish
- Onions
- Chives
- Avocados
- Uncooked eggs
- Milk
- Raisins
- Grapes
- Alcohol
- Coffee
- Oranges
- Macadamia nuts

147

TUBBY TABBY WEIGHS IN

I love my big, huggable cat, Leo, but my friends joke about his size. They call him Leo the Large and ask me if I really have two cats, not one. He is 8 years old and weighs 16 pounds. I tell my friends he is just big-boned, but I know he is overweight. He doesn't seem to have any health problems, though. What's wrong with having a chubby cat?

Plenty. And sadly, Leo has plenty of feline company. An estimated 60 percent of cats in the United States tip the scales as overweight or obese, according to the Association for Pet Obesity Prevention. A decade ago, that percentage was less than 50, so chubby cats are increasing in both number and size.

Overweight cats are at more risk for diabetes, heart disease, arthritis, kidney disease, and a host of other conditions. As their bellies expand, they are less motivated to do anything beyond eating, sleeping, and making the occasional trip to the litter box. They often drink less water, which makes them likelier candidates for stones in their urine or for urinary tract infections. And they are unable to reach all spots on their bodies, especially the back and the rear to properly groom and avoid infections and skin conditions.

Let's help Leo slim down smartly. Take a "before" photo of him and put it in a visible place such as your refrigerator door. Start a food diary and weigh Leo once every three days. If you keep his food bowl always full, cease. Ask your veterinarian for advice on a high-quality diet food (some have more fiber, which helps the cat feel fuller).

To downsize Leo, you need to start sizing up his meal portions so you know exactly how much food you are giving him. Use an actual measuring cup, not a plastic deli container or other imprecise scoop. Set up specific mealtimes. Spread out his kibble on a cookie sheet instead of a bowl. It will take him longer to eat his chow.

Work with your veterinarian on slowly decreasing Leo's food portions. You don't want to cut back too quickly. In cats, the dangers of crash dieting can lead to hepatic lipidosis, more commonly known as fatty liver disease.

Your goal is for Leo to lose a few ounces per week, so that the excess weight comes off gradually and doesn't return. As the ounces start to melt, bring out the inner kitten in Leo by encouraging him to play and move around more. If you have stairs, put a low-calorie treat like shaved bonito fish

flakes at the top of the stairs when Leo is at the bottom. Show him the treat and call him up. Drag a toy on a string for him to chase. Buy him an interactive toy that will engage his attention when you are away.

Each month, take a progress photo of Leo. Within six months or so, your friends will be calling him Leo the Lean. 🐾

feline fact

Some cats love eating cantaloupe because many of the amino acids in meat can also be found in cantaloupe.

DRINK UP, KITTY, PLEASE

In our multi-pet household, we have a couple of water bowls— one in the kitchen and one in the den. We always see our two dogs happily lapping up the water, but rarely see our cat, Clancy, drinking water. He seems healthy, but what can I do to encourage him to drink more?

Rare is the cat who races to the water bowl and laps it dry like most dogs do. Two leading reasons are ancestry and physiology. Today's domestic cats are descendants of cats who hailed from the desert plains of Mesopotamia. And cats require less water consumption to stay hydrated than their canine pals. An average 10-pound indoor cat needs 7 to 10 ounces of water each day to keep his skin and organs well hydrated.

First, I applaud you for noticing that Clancy is not a big water drinker. You are paying attention to his daily routine and will be more tuned in to early signs of any health or behavior issue.

One of my friends is renowned animal trainer Samantha Martin who motivates her Amazing Acro-Cats to

ring bells, jump through hoops, leap over hurdles, and do other tricks onstage before sold-out audiences (see Strays Turned Stars, page 112). But even Samantha knows her cat-training limits. Like us, she can lead a cat to water but she can't make it drink.

What's the solution? For starters, feeding Clancy a canned food diet is an excellent way to sneak in more water each day. Canned food is between 70 and 80 percent water.

Serve water in wide, stainless steel bowls. Most cats do not like to have their whiskers scrunched inside narrow, deep water bowls. Avoid using water bowls made of plastic, as some cats are sensitive to plastic and can develop skin allergies over time. They can also harbor harmful bacteria and chemicals that can leach into the water.

Add a third water bowl accessible only to Clancy, not your dogs. Add a few teaspoons of flavored favorites, such as tuna juice (water based) or sodium-free chicken broth, to the water. Make sure the broth does not contain onions or garlic.

Try adding a little "motion to the ocean" by introducing Clancy to a pet drinking fountain that circulates water in a bowl. Many cats seem to prefer fresh, running water. Some cats can't resist the drip-drip from a kitchen or bathroom faucet. If you go with the faucet option, set time limits so you don't have a sky-high water bill.

Yes, our felines are fussy sippers, but I am rooting for you to transition Clancy into getting the fluids he needs each day to keep him happy and hydrated. 🐾

MAKING A SPLASH

I swear my cat is part raccoon! Chloe insists on putting her paws in her water bowl. Sometimes she splashes around without taking a drink. She also makes a mess at mealtime by pawing some of her food out of the bowl and scattering it on the kitchen floor. She doesn't always eat these spilled pieces of food, and I'm forever cleaning up her messes. Can I change her behavior?

In spite of their reputation for tolerating only dry land, many cats are actually water lovers. Some, such as Chloe, like to play in standing water, whereas others are fascinated by running water and prefer to drink from a faucet. There are

a lot of theories as well as urban legends about this behavior, but no one knows the reason for sure. This attraction to running water may reflect an adaptive behavior from a wild past. Perhaps because running water has fewer contaminants, many wild animals prefer to drink from streams rather than ponds.

Chloe's paw splashing could also be attributed to her need to test the water to make sure it is safe. The paw pad represents one of the most sensitive areas on a cat's body. Chloe is scooping water with her paw to check for possible "dangers" in the water or to test the temperature. Cats' long-distance eyesight is superb and they see anything moving easily, but their close-up vision is somewhat weak. They rely on their noses to sample food and paws to test water. And she may be partaking in a little fun and enjoying seeing the ripples her paw creates in the bowl.

Please make sure that you provide Chloe with fresh water every day, even if she makes a mess. Offer her more than one bowl in your home. If you don't mind her perching on a bathroom sink, leave one with a few inches of water for her to play in during the day. You might consider an inexpensive automatic water dispenser that trickles water continuously. Many cats find these irresistible. They are readily available at pet supply stores and online.

Another idea is to take a one-gallon plastic jug and cut a hole about two inches from the bottom. Make the hole just a bit bigger than Chloe's head (don't forget to allow for her whiskers!) so that she can reach in for a drink but can't splash too much water on the floor. If she pushes the jug around, you can attach it to a wall.

As for Chloe's messy eating habit, first rule out any possible dental problems. Some cats with bad teeth or inflamed gums have difficulty chewing and swallowing kibble. Make sure Chloe's teeth and gums are healthy. If she checks out okay, then let me offer some suggestions.

Your cat might be bored with the same old chow every day. You can warm up dry food slightly to bring out a more beckoning aroma, or you can make chowtime a bit of an adventure. Like you, I had a cat who seemed to take great delight in flinging her food around. I placed kibble in small piles in the kitchen and dining room for Samantha to stalk, find, and consume. She had fun conquering her kibble and seemed quite satisfied with the arrangement.

Try this with Chloe and praise her as she finds and eats her "prey." She may be more apt to get into the "hunt" of the food and less apt to toss the food around. Puzzle and treat balls that you fill with kibble might solve the problem, too.

To contain the mess, forget placemats. They are simply too small. Opt instead for a large plastic drain board or tray with a rim to prevent food from spreading across the floor. Or supersize the protected area with a plastic tablecloth that you can place on the kitchen floor during mealtime. You can easily take the tablecloth outside to shake out excess crumbs and clean it with a sponge. Then just fold it and tuck it in the pantry or closet until the next meal.

Finally, pay attention to what you serve the meals in. Some cats have definite preferences. Some like ceramic or steel better than plastic, which can impart an off odor or taste. Many prefer bowls with wide enough openings so that their whiskers don't touch the sides when they eat. Try serving Chloe's food in a wide-mouthed ceramic bowl if you are now using a plastic one. It may turn her into a neater eater. 🐾

feline fact

Just like a person's fingerprint, a cat's nose pad sports a unique pattern of ridges.

PASS THE GREENS, PLEASE

Maybe my cat is part cow! Maggie is a black-and-white cat, about 3 years old, whom I've had since she was a kitten. She is an indoor cat who loves to safely explore our fenced backyard in her harness and leash. When she is out in the yard, Maggie makes a beeline for the lawn and starts munching away. Sometimes she eats a lot only to vomit up the blades of grass later on. Is she okay, and why does she seem to like grass?

Many cats dig greens, even though they are true carnivores. Eating grass is actually a fairly common activity among felines, who have a natural instinct to supplement their dietary needs with plant material. Veterinary nutritionists report that an all-meat diet does not provide certain vitamins and minerals that cats seem to know are found in grass and greens.

A second possible reason Maggie heads for the lawn is because the blades

of grass serve to help oust hairballs and to settle upset stomachs. Yes, the result is a gross puddle (hopefully on the linoleum, not the carpet), but Maggie understands the power of Mother Nature.

I caution you to steer Maggie away from the lawn if you use any kind of chemicals or pesticides. Instead, treat Maggie to an indoor patch of organically grown lawn in your house. Grass is easy to grow and it sprouts quickly. Better yet, grow fresh catnip for Maggie. This hardy herb is easy to grow from seeds. Just set the pot in a dark, damp area to allow the seeds to sprout and then relocate the pot to a sunny spot. I recommend a place where Maggie likes to sun herself, perhaps near a window in the living room.

You can also consult your veterinarian about providing Maggie with a commercial hairball preventive. Regularly grooming her with your dampened hands (not dripping wet, just enough to collect loose hair) can help remove dead hairs from Maggie's coat and may reduce her hairball episodes. 🐾

Poisonous Plant Inventory

Take an inventory of the plants in your home and yard to make sure that none of them are poisonous to your gotta-have-greens feline. Different parts of a plant—leaves, seeds, berries, roots, or bark—may be deadly to felines. Landing on the top 10 list of common plants toxic to cats are lilies, sago palm, aloe, kalanchoe, cyclamen, oleander, amaryllis, corn plant (dracaena), begonias, and tulips.

For a complete list, please visit the ASPCA's Animal Poison Control Center's website (aspca.org/apcc) or call 1-888-426-4435. If you suspect your cat has nibbled on a poisonous plant, take the cat and the plant with you to the veterinary clinic—pronto—to confirm the plant's identification.

You can feel safe in beautifying your home and garden with these feline-friendly plants: alyssum, cape jasmine, dwarf aster, garden marigold, German violet, honeysuckle fuchsia, Jacob's ladder, pansy orchid, and summer hyacinth.

lily

sago palm

aloe

kalanchoe

cyclamen

oleander

amaryllis

dracaena

begonias

tulips

THE ABCS OF CBD FOR CATS

I have found that CBD oils ease stress and arthritic pain in my shoulders and hips. My cat is about to celebrate his tenth birthday. Is it safe to give him CBD, too?

Cannabidiol (CBD) is one of the active ingredients in cannabis plants. CBD oil is derived from hemp but does not have a psychoactive effect. That's because CBD oil does not contain tetrahydrocannabinol (THC)—the psychoactive compound that produces a "high." Medical cannibis is legal in many US states, but the FDA has approved only one CBD product for use in humans: a prescription drug for some rare forms of epilepsy.

The explosive popularity in the use of CBD by people looking for ways to ease anxiety, pain, and other issues in themselves is now finding its way into treats, soft chews, sprays, tinctures, and capsules for their cats. What could be good for us could be good for our cats, right?

For now, the answer from veterinarians and health experts is a big "maybe." There are lots of anecdotal success stories but no veterinary studies proving that CBD will improve a cat's appetite, ease arthritic pain, slow down dementia, or reduce stress during car rides and veterinary visits. And the Food and Drug Administration has not yet approved cannabis products for pets.

Keep in mind that feline livers process medications differently than human or canine livers. The feline physiology is far more sensitive than ours. You need to be cautious when introducing a CBD treat to your cat, especially if your cat is susceptible to digestive upset or itching due to food sensitivities. Consider these guidelines before you decide.

- Seek your veterinarian's advice before you give any CBD product to your cat. As far as veterinarians know, CBD oil does not interfere with other medications because the endocannabinoid system does not use the same pathways in the body as other medications. But talk with your veterinarian. It is important to use CBD oil safely as you would any other drug.

- Recognize that a little goes a long way in dosing. When it comes to using CBD oil on cats, more is not better. Appropriate concentration is key. For a high-quality product, you may only need a couple of drops in your cat's mouth.

- Don't be a bargain hunter. High-quality CBD products are not cheap. Liposomes are the carriers of hemp oil that act as delivery agents in the body. It costs a lot of money to produce them at a decent level.

- Seek products with certificate of analysis (COA) approval provided by an independent third-party tester. This verifies the product is free of pesticides and heavy metals and that it contains what it says it does. If the product does not have a COA, you have no idea what is in there.

- Watch out for cure claims. Avoid products that claim they are the best or promise to "cure" or "treat" specific health conditions on their packaging or websites. These are illegal claims because they have not been approved by the FDA.

- Keep an eye on your cat when you begin dosing with CBD. Cannabidiol can cause gastrointestinal upset and some sedation, which goes away if you stop using it. Because we don't know much about the side effects in cats yet, watch for any changes in your pet while using CBD.

Here are a couple of resources for learning more about CBD oil and cats. The Veterinary Cannabis Education and Consulting group, founded by Casara Andre, DVM, offers online education and consulting on the use of cannabis in pets. Another organization is the Veterinary Cannabis Society, which brings together veterinarians, pet parents, and cannabis industry representatives to advocate for knowledge about and appropriate use of cannabis treatment for animals. 🐾

UH-OH, IT'S PILL TIME!

My cat, Tiger, was diagnosed with inflammatory bowel disease (IBS) and I now need to give him a pill every day. I know that the medicine will make him feel better, but he seems to have a sixth sense about when I plan to give him medicine, and then he runs and hides. How can he know it is pill time? And how can I safely give him his daily dose?

Your responsibility role for Tiger just advanced a big step. It can be challenging to pill a cat. Up to 40 percent of people fail to comply with instructions on medicating their pets. The main reason? It's too much of a hassle. Felines can be notorious for hiding when it is medication time. Others put up a fight or try to wiggle free. And some have mastered the ability to spit out the pill, stare at you, and then dash away.

Consider pill time from Tiger's standpoint. The pill probably doesn't taste good, and he certainly doesn't enjoy being held tight and having his mouth pried open.

Consult your veterinarian to see if Tiger's pills can be formulated into feline favorite flavors, such as tuna, chicken, or salmon. If it won't compromise the potency of the medicine, ask your veterinarian if you can crush the pill into a spoonful of canned food or human baby food (make sure the baby food does not contain onions or garlic) to make it more palatable. He may also take it hidden in a tasty "pill pocket" or mixed into a small spoonful of yogurt or a dab of cream cheese or butter.

If these suggestions aren't possible, try my yum-yuck-yum pill-giving method. Cats are masters at reading our moods and intentions. So before reaching for Tiger's pill bottle, put yourself in the right frame of mind. Be patient but purposeful. Don't be anxious or agitated, and definitely don't try to give him his pill when you're in a rush.

Before approaching Tiger, place everything you need in your bathroom: the pill, a dab of butter, a thick towel, and two small, yummy treats. Coat the pill with butter to make it taste better and to help it slip down his throat. The bathroom is ideal because it is small and you can close the door to prevent Tiger from escaping.

Time the pill-giving for when Tiger is not eating or grooming or using the litter box. Cradle him calmly in your arms as you take him into the bathroom. Speak in a soft, confident tone. Give him one of the treats—yum!

Now for the yuck step. Wrap Tiger in a towel so that his paws are contained but his head is uncovered. Hold the pill between your thumb and index finger as you gently tilt his head up with your other hand. That should cause his jaw to open so you can place the buttered pill in the back of his throat. Close his mouth, blow on his nose, and stroke his chin to cause him to swallow.

Let him out of the towel and reward him with a second treat—yum again!

Before you open the door, inspect the floor to make sure he did not manage to spit out the pill. Then let Tiger walk or dash out on his own. Count a few seconds before you exit and head for the recliner to watch TV or grab a book. You want to communicate to him that pill time is not a big deal and that you are not chasing after him.

Remember to speak in upbeat tones and to breathe in and out deeply to keep your body from tensing. Avoid rushing or saying phrases like "I'm sorry" as cats are adept at reading our emotional states. Giving medicine to our pets will never rank among our favorite activities but remind yourself that you are doing a noble job taking care of your cat. 🐾

Toxic Tragedies

Curiosity can kill a cat, especially if she accidentally swallows human medications, including over-the-counter ones. Topping the lethal list are acetaminophen, aspirin, and ibuprofen. Others include nonprescription medicines to fight diarrhea such as Kaopectate and stomach settlers such as Pepto-Bismol. Be careful not to drop or spill them when you're dispensing some for yourself!

GROOMER TO THE RESCUE

My cat, Jimmy, is 12 years old. I've had him since he was a kitten. He is a shorthaired ginger tabby. I've never really thought much about his coat because he seems to keep it clean and tidy. But lately, I've noticed that my other cat, Karma, who is 6, has begun to groom Jimmy. She licks his head, inside his ears, and even the base of his tail. I thought cats were solitary creatures. Can you explain why Karma is grooming Jimmy?

Contrary to the popular but misguided notion that cats are loners, they frequently form close social bonds. Jimmy and Karma share the same home, the same owner. They are part of a harmonious colony. Touch is an important way in which they communicate with one another.

Karma is displaying her affection for her senior brother by assisting him in keeping his coat clean and healthy. Cats who spend a lot of time together, especially indoor cats who get along, will often engage in this type of "you scratch my back, I'll scratch yours" activity. It solidifies their social bond. Social grooming, known as allogrooming, is common in more than 40 species of animals, including rats, deer, dogs, monkeys, and cattle. In addition to the social aspect, these animals groom one another to treat wounds, tame tensions, and oust bugs such as fleas.

Even though it is sweet that Karma is tending to the grooming needs of Jimmy, I urge you to keep tabs on him. If Jimmy is not grooming himself at all anymore, he may be coping with a medical condition that needs attention. Without Karma stepping in to assist, there is a good chance that Jimmy's coat would become dry, dull, and full of dandruff. 🐾

The At-Home Wellness Check

In my pet first aid classes I teach people how to do head-to-tail wellness checks, think like a pet detective, and identify clues that their cat is not 100 percent healthy. Tap in to your senses and look, listen, smell, and safely touch to catch early signs of illness or injury.

I recommend getting into the habit of a weekly wellness check. Select a time and place where you and your cat are relaxed and can be together free of any distractions.

1. Start with the head. The nose should be slightly moist, without any discharge, or dry but not cracked. The eyes should be clear and free of any discharge, and the pupils should be symmetrical. Use a small treat to test if your pet moves his eyes to follow it. Check the ears, inside and out, and sniff. Ear infections often smell like dirty socks! Gently rub the sides of the muzzle and top of the head to check for suspicious lumps, cuts, or bumps.

2. Assess the neck and spine. You can do this with your cat standing or lying down. Gently hold his head in your palms and rotate his neck left and right. Then place one hand on his neck and glide the other hand down his spine all the way to the base of the tail. Note if he winces or if you spot any cuts, bumps, or masses.

3. Check that your cat's breathing is smooth, rhythmic, and easy.

4. Palpate the abdomen. Gently press with your open palms for any signs of pain. Check the nipples for swelling or tenderness. Examine the genitals and make sure that the anal area is free of any old feces, dried urine, dirt, or hair.

5. Survey the coat. Your cat's coat should be shiny and clean, without excessive shedding, odor, or bald patches.

6. Support your standing cat with one hand while you use your other hand to examine each leg and to test his range of motion. Then examine each paw and in between the toes for ticks, foxtails, or other foreign bodies and check that the claws are not overgrown. Make sure the paw pads are not red or cut or torn.

7. End with the tail. Long or short, fluffy or smooth, all feline tails contain numerous small bones. Run your closed hand gently down the tail, feeling for signs of pain, limited range of use, or cuts.

At the end of each session, reward your cat with his favorite treat. This will motivate him or her to be cooperative during your weekly wellness exams. This should be a fun, bonding time for you both!

YUCK! HAIRBALLS!

My longhaired cat, Nala, seems to groom her beautiful coat all the time. She is an indoor cat nearing her fifth birthday. At least once or twice a week, I can count on finding a hairball coughed up on the carpet. She never seems to pick floors that are easy to clean, like the tile in the kitchen. She gets regular checkups, and my veterinarian has not found any health problems. So why the hairballs?

It's an inescapable feline fact: Hairballs happen. It doesn't matter if the cat is a longhaired Ragdoll or a sleek Siamese, a kitten or a senior cat. Hairballs don't discriminate based on age or breed. Longhaired cats and those felines who tend to overgroom themselves are more prone to these yucky expulsions.

The scientific name for a hairball is *trichobezoar*, but it remains a hairy, matted mess expelled from your cat's stomach. When Nala uses her barbed tongue across her body to lift and remove excess hair, that hair glides down her intestinal tract and, if all goes according to plan, sails out with poop deposits in the litter box. But if the hair doesn't move along the digestive tract properly, it can collect and eventually has to come out the other direction.

Hairballs are fairly common, but a cat can go days, weeks, or months without hacking up one. A healthy hairball is cigar-shaped and matches the color of the cat's fur. An unhealthy one emits a foul odor or contains a foreign body like perhaps a piece of fabric from a cat toy. If the hairball looks like it contains coffee grounds, that could be dried blood, a life-threatening situation that warrants a prompt veterinary visit.

I also urge you to consult with your veterinarian if Nala displays any of these warning signs:

- Increase in the frequency of hairballs
- Makes dry hacking sounds
- Displays a swollen abdomen

- Coat becomes dry and matted
- Constipation

You can help Nala show off her healthy coat and reduce her hairball incidents by brushing and combing her daily. (Brush shorthaired cats twice a week using a slicker brush.) Grooming also aids in spotting any skin or coat problems such as lumps or bumps or fleas and ticks, removes dead skin, and minimizes matting. You can also treat her to an appointment at a pet-grooming salon on a regular basis.

Practice preventive measures by giving Nala hairball-control treats and digestive-aid supplements. You can also add a teaspoon or two of canned pumpkin (not the sugar-filled pie filling, though) to her meal a few times a week. You can also grow kitty grass indoors for Nala to munch on. 🐾

CREATE A GLAMOUR PUSS

Our family recently acquired a lovely new cat named Princess, who has beautiful, long, gray fur. I love the longhaired look, but her coat tangles easily and she has several mats on her flanks and belly. I had been assuming that she would groom herself, but I now realize I need to help. I tried to comb her a few times, but I must have tugged too much and she hissed. Now when I approach her with a brush and comb in hand, she glares, runs, and hides. What can I do to make grooming time a more pleasant experience?

Cats usually do a good job of grooming themselves, but they can all benefit from the assistance of a person with a brush. Longhaired cats and cats with very fine, fluffy fur can easily turn into matted, bedraggled ragamuffins without regular, even daily, attention. In the spring and fall, when many cats shed more than usual, a little extra grooming from their human pals helps keep them looking their best.

After your first sessions with Princess, she relates the brush and comb with hair-pulling pain—no wonder she flees from you. And you are probably feeling hesitant and reluctant to approach her, giving her more reason to think that something is wrong. Time to regroup. Have you ever taken a yoga or meditation class? Remember the lessons on deep inhales and exhales from your diaphragm? Be calm and take deep breaths when you are working with Princess. If you are relaxed, she will sense that you don't want to hurt her.

Start your first few grooming sessions by just talking sweetly to Princess and gently stroking her coat from the top of the head to the tail. Move slowly and steadily, and back off if she tries to move away or seems tense. As she relaxes, her purr machine should engage. Use this time to finger gently through her fur for mats, lumps, bumps, cuts, or

evidence of fleas. For the first few days, stop your grooming session here. You are rebuilding Princess's trust in you.

For your next sessions, arm yourself with the right tools: a mat-splitter, a slicker brush, and a wide-toothed comb. A mat-splitter glides through mats and tangles easier and more safely than a pair of scissors because the razor blade is shielded. A slicker brush will make her coat lie flat. For long fur, cat-grooming experts recommend a wide-toothed or shedding comb specifically designed to get rid of the dead undercoat hairs that cause tangles. For a fine, silky coat, you may want to add a grooming glove designed to smooth the coat and cause it to glimmer.

Remove mats by holding them away from the skin and using the mat-splitter to cut them out. Use the slicker brush to remove loose hair and to smooth the coat. Next, lift the coat away from the body with a wide-toothed comb to add beautiful fullness. (To prevent matting, most longhaired cats with fine coats need to be combed every day, taking the comb to the roots.) Finish with the grooming glove for extra polish.

Use flowing strokes on Princess with the wide-toothed comb, moving in the direction of the hair growth. Start at the head and work down toward the tail and then the legs. Take a break and pet Princess and perhaps give her a taste of her favorite treat. If she struggles, let her leave and try again the next day.

Don't expect to completely comb out her fur in one session. Be content to attack just one or two mats a day until they are all gone.

Set aside 5 minutes each day to become your cat's personal groomer. Pick times when you are both relaxed— in the evenings when you watch television or read a book or in the morning when you wake up and Princess is still a bit sleepy and hungry. Use her empty tummy to your advantage and reward her good grooming behavior with treats. In no time, Princess will look forward to these glamour sessions with you.

If Princess is afflicted with lots of mats or there are any mats too close to the skin for a mat-splitter, you might want to take her to a professional groomer first and get her coat in ship-shape condition, then you can follow up with daily at-home care. Don't neglect a longhaired cat—small mats can turn into tough tangles that may need to be shaved off.

A final tip: Longhaired cats can benefit greatly from regular bathing because their coats retain body oils and dust, which aggravates the matting problem. A bath also removes dead hair better than combing. Your cat will not only have to become used to the bath process but blow-drying as well. Using a quiet, medium-speed, moderate-heat blower works well—most cats eventually come to love the warmth. It is a noisy dryer they dislike. 🐾

Mat Attack!

Why give your cat the brush-off? Here are several good reasons.

- Your sofa and clothing won't reveal evidence of your hairy, shedding feline(s).

- You can enjoy some true quality time with your cat.

- Your cat is less likely to cough up nasty hairballs.

- You can discover lumps, rashes, and other skin-related health problems early for quicker (and hopefully less expensive) veterinary treatment.

- You can deal with mats in long fur when they are small.

Conquer mats in longhaired coats by using a wide-toothed comb. Start by carefully pulling apart the mat with your fingers or use a mat-splitter as much as you can. Holding the mat at the base, gently but firmly work out the mess by starting at the tip and working in toward the base with the comb. Using scissors sounds like a quick solution, but I advise against it because you risk accidentally cutting your cat's skin. For any mats you cannot comb out on your own, please seek help from a professional cat groomer.

NAIL KNOW-HOW

When I pick up my cat, she sinks her sharp, long nails into my shoulder and neck. It hurts. Even though she is an indoor cat, I don't plan on having her declawed. How can I keep her nails trimmed and save my skin from her scratches?

Just like us, cats benefit from regular mani-pedi sessions. Overgrown nails can get snapped on the carpet or curl and grow back into the skin. Both are painful scenarios that can be avoided with regular nail trims. My cats, Mikey, Rusty, and Casey, sport all of their claws and easily accept having their nails clipped on a regular basis. I cheerfully call out to them, *It's mani-pedi time* and usher each one at a time into my bathroom to be their purr-sonal manicurist. I speak in a calm voice, take my time, and, of course, offer them plenty of yummy treats to make this a welcoming experience.

To help you survive nail-trimming time, you need to think like a cat. They are capable of controlling the claw movements, making them extend or retract. Start by playing with your cat's

feet regularly to get her used to someone touching her toes. Gently squeeze the footpads to expose the nails. Do this whenever you are petting her or grooming her.

When you are ready to do an actual trim, set out the tools you will need: nail trimmers designed for cats, a thick towel, and styptic powder (just in case you clip the nail too short and it bleeds). Then bring your cat into the bathroom and give her a small treat to start the proceedings on a good note. Be upbeat. Silly as it sounds, try singing a happy tune. Don't worry if you're off-key—your cat won't tell your friends. Or at least talk soothingly as you work. Sitting on the floor or in a chair, hold your cat with her back against you so that you

can hold a paw in one hand and use the clippers with the other.

If your cat struggles too much in this position or tries to scratch, wrap her in a thick towel, exposing her head and her one front paw. Hold the paw steady in one hand. Position your thumb on top of the paw and your other fingers underneath and gently press to expose the nails. Snip the tip of each nail, including the dewclaw on the side. Just nip off the white part, being careful to avoid the vein that runs into each claw. Having a partner can be very helpful with this process—one to hold and one to clip.

Tune in to your cat's reaction. If she starts to kick up a fuss, then just do one paw this time. You don't want to turn a routine chore into a battle royal. See if a yummy treat will settle her down before you start on the next paw. If she's very upset, wait and do the second paw the next day. Patience is your ally. Depending on your cat, you will need to trim nails every two to four weeks, so your goal is to make nail trimming seem ho-hum to your cat. Remember to heap on the praise during the trim session.

If you accidentally clip too deep and nick the quick, it will bleed. That's where the styptic powder comes in. Just apply a dab of powder on the nail for a few seconds and apply pressure until the bleeding stops. 🐾

The Ins and Outs of Cat Claws

Claws, like human fingernails, are made of keratin, but instead of growing in a nailbed, they are extensions of the bone and contain blood and nerve endings. Rather than growing longer, claws grow in layers, like an onion. When cats "sharpen" their claws, what they are actually doing is pulling off the worn-down outer layer to reveal the pointed tip.

Cats depend on the five claws on each front paw and the four claws on each of their back legs for numerous uses.

- To grip while climbing
- To defend themselves in a fight
- To hold on to captured prey, be that a real or toy mouse
- To mark territory by scratching and releasing scent
- To dig in the litter box to cover up their waste

We often say that cats have retractable claws, when actually they are *protractible*. Most of the time, the claws naturally retract into the pads of the toes. To extend or protract them, the cat tightens tendons in the toe to reveal the sharp tips.

Declawing a cat is drastic surgery that involves removing the tip of the toe bone and severing those tendons. Recovery is painful and may result in permanent behavioral changes. The procedure is banned in many European countries and many North American veterinarians refuse to perform it.

BATH? NO, THANKS!

My dog, Max, is a gentle bullmastiff who loves to swim and take baths. My cat, Star, definitely resists getting wet. I have to bathe her occasionally, though, because Max tends to slobber on her and she smells like a dog. Why do cats hate baths so much?

Cats spend many waking hours grooming themselves so they can look and smell so feline fine. They would never be caught in public wearing a dirty T-shirt or clothes that clashed. They like sporting clean, well-groomed coats. That must be why cats with black-and-white coats are fondly referred to as tuxedo cats—not Oreo cookie cats.

While a flea invasion or an encounter with a skunk or some sticky or oily substance necessitates human intervention, most cats never need to be bathed at all.

A good brushing (daily for fluffy felines and less frequently for shorter-coated cats) helps keep skin and fur healthy. Unless Star is regularly drenched with dog drool, let her take care of the problem herself with self-grooming. If she is still stinky, try using a dry cat shampoo or unscented, alcohol-free wipes rather than subjecting her to a full-fledged bath.

As for the notion that cats take to water like oil to vinegar, that statement does not in fact hold water. Some wild felines such as tigers and ocelots cool down from the jungle heat by swimming or enter water to hunt fish and other aquatic creatures. Corky, my childhood cat, loved to swim with our dogs in our backyard lake and would follow anyone holding a fishing pole in hopes of landing a bluegill dinner. Many show cats enjoy regular baths before competing for blue ribbons.

If you do feel that Star needs a bath, follow these tips.

- Give her a mani-pedi before the bath. Clipping the nail tips can keep you from being scratched. Comb or brush out dead hair before bathing to avoid clumps and mats.

- Stock the bathroom ahead of time with thick towels, washcloths, treats, your cat's carrier, a blow dryer, and a cup. Use good-quality cat shampoos and conditioners that are free of harsh detergents. Select ones with vitamin D and enzymes that boost healthy skin cells.

- Don the right attire. Go with long sleeves and, depending on your cat's catitude, protective gloves. I like to set the mood by playing classical music or singing a happy tune by modifying that classic Bobby Darin song, "Splish, splash, I was bathing a cat!" Provide plenty of praise and treats (if she'll eat them) during the process.

- Always bathe your cat in a sink, never a bathtub. A tub is too big and allows more escape opportunities. Plus, it is a real pain having to bend over. Place a nonskid mat in the sink. Put a little warm water in and gently place your cat's feet in.

- Hold your cat from underneath, with your hand coming between her front legs to support her chest. Make sure she is facing AWAY from you to minimize being scratched.

- Never submerge your cat—it is too scary. And besides, your cat didn't sign up for swimming lessons. Avoid spray nozzles, too. Instead, wet and rinse the coat using cups of warm water. Use a warm, wet washcloth to clean the face.

- Towel dry. Some cats will tolerate being inside a top-loading carrier on the counter. Direct warm air on a low setting from a handheld blow dryer to dry the coat. Keep your cat in the warm bathroom with you until her coat is mostly dry. Give her treats while you brush her coat.

When you're all done, open the door and let your cat race out of the bathroom without trying to hold or pet her. Give her a little time to settle down, and see if she doesn't strut a bit once she's used to her new look! 🐾

TAKING IT UNDER THE CHIN

I was scratching my 3-year-old cat, William, under his chin recently when I felt some scabby bumps and noticed flakes of what looked like dirt. I know he doesn't have fleas, and he takes good care of his coat. I was afraid that he might have mange or even skin cancer, but my veterinarian diagnosed it as feline acne. I've never heard of this condition. Can you tell me more about it?

Teenagers aren't the only ones who develop acne—some cats do, too. Medically speaking, feline acne is a keratinization disorder, which is a fancy way of saying that pores under the chin become blocked with cellular debris, causing blackheads. Left untreated, these clogged pores can become swollen and infected. They eventually rupture and create bloodied scabs, raised lesions, and patches of baldness. Cats with white chins may look like they have goatees.

Veterinary experts do not know what causes this condition or how prevalent it is among the feline population. Popular theories point to heightened stress, use of plastic feeding bowls, fleabites, a genetic predisposition, or allergies as possible triggers. Feline acne can appear just once then disappear forever, or it can last for the cat's entire lifetime.

Controlling feline acne requires working closely with your veterinarian and possibly a veterinary dermatologist. There are a variety of treatments available, from over-the-counter ointments to prescription medications, but the trick is finding which one works best on your cat. Here is a rundown of common treatments for feline acne.

Flea comb. Run the comb gently under the chin on a daily basis to lift and remove dried scabs and blackhead flecks.

Medicated acne pad. Dab your cat's chin once or twice a day to keep the blackheads on the chin from worsening. Let the area air-dry.

Epsom salts compress. Hold a warm compress on the chin for 3 to 5 minutes a day to dry out the area and to reduce inflammation. Then apply vitamin A ointment to repair damaged skin cells.

Prescription shampoo. Apply this with warm compresses to cleanse and exfoliate dead skin in the chin area. Check with your veterinarian for dosage instructions.

Benzoyl peroxide gel. This prescription medication typically contains 2.5 to 3 percent benzoyl peroxide that penetrates deeply into the hair follicles to remove blackheads. Caution: The peroxide can bleach fabric if the treated cat rubs his chin against the furniture or carpeting.

Oral antibiotics. Your veterinarian may prescribe medication in pill or liquid form if the acne becomes infected.

My veterinarian friends offer one final bit of advice: Do not squeeze any pimple under your cat's chin—you risk causing an infection. 🐾

feline fact

The main reasons a cat develops itchy skin are allergic reactions, fleas and other parasites, diseases such as diabetes and hyperthyroidism, a dry environment, poor diet, poor grooming, and bacterial or fungal infections.

173

Petting with a Purpose

One of the best ways to communicate with our cats is through touch. Most cats love to be stroked, petted, and scratched. Most people enjoy the feel of that silky fur and the sight of a happy, purring face. When properly performed, the power of touch delivers many therapeutic and health benefits. I like to call massage "petting with a purpose."

Emotionally, massage strengthens the people-pet bond, helps curb aggression and other unwanted behaviors, and improves a cat's sociability with people and animals. Massage also plays a role in chronic conditions such as arthritis. Although not a cure, massage reduces joint stiffness and pain by delivering oxygenated blood to trouble spots.

Regularly massaged cats become accustomed to being handled. They associate touch with positive experiences. That can take the stress out of combing and brushing, nail trimming, car trips, veterinarian visits, and cat breed shows for both the cat and the owner.

Some Dos and Don'ts of Cat Massage

- O Do approach your cat slowly and speak in a soothing tone.

- O Do use clean hands—no need for oils, creams, or lotions.

- O Do pay attention to feedback. Look for purring, rolling onto one side, kneading, and soft eye blinking. Stop your massage if your cat squirms away from you, hisses, sinks his back under your hand, or meows in protest. You don't want him to resort to biting or scratching.

- O Do repeat a technique your cat likes.

- O Don't force a massage on your cat.

- O Don't massage your cat when you feel stressed or hurried.

- O Don't press too deeply—you could harm your cat.

- O Don't substitute massage for medical treatment for conditions such as arthritis. Let it complement the care plan devised by your veterinarian.

Cat Massage Techniques

All thumbs? When it comes to cat massage, first practice these six motions on a pillow or stuffed toy cat before trying them on your cat.

Go with the glide. This classic massage stroke is simply a straight, flowing, continuous motion. Move your fingers or palm from the top of the head down the back to the tail.

Create circles. Move your fingertips in clockwise or counterclockwise circles about the size of half-dollars.

Do the wave. Make side-to-side rocking strokes with open palm and flat fingers (mimic the movements of a windshield wiper).

Focus on flicking. Pretend that you are lightly brushing imaginary crumbs off a table. You can flick with one, two, or three fingers.

Use the real rub. Move along your cat's body slowly, exerting feather-light, light, and mild pressures. See which she responds to the best.

Heed the knead. This gentle caress uses an open-and-shut motion of your palm and all five fingers. It is ideal for the spine area.

The Ins and Outs of Life with
MODERN CATS

Times are changing for the better for our feline friends. A generation or two ago, plenty of cats were described as barn cats, mousers, or friendly strays. Far too few family cats saw veterinarians for even a yearly examination.

Happily, a let's-embrace-felines revolution is under way. Today, it is cool to be a cat. And it is cool to hang out with cats. Cats of today are Instagram stars, feline fashionistas, adventure cats, road-trip companions, therapy tabbies, and motivators for home renovation and design. Our growing connection to and better understanding of cats have led to the creation of cat cafés, catios, and even dating apps for cat lovers.

It is becoming the norm for cats to be part of the "in" crowd, meaning they live happily inside our homes rather than roaming unsupervised around the neighborhood. We now recognize the importance of providing mental and physical enrichment to homebody cats by providing them with cat trees that may look like jungle gyms, toys and food puzzles, and litter boxes designed to meet their wants and needs, not our preferences.

Look around and you will see more cats walking the neighborhood on leashes and harnesses, riding in pet strollers at pet-welcoming events, or even surveying the scenery on a hike with their favorite people from the vantage point of a specially designed kitty backpack.

In this section, I am delighted to open your eyes to the opportunities awaiting twenty-first-century cats, indoors and outdoors. It has never been a better time to be a cat. Me-WOW!

GIVE ME A C FOR CATIO

My two indoor cats love sitting on window perches and watching outdoor activities, from flying birds to dogs walked on sidewalks to my comings and goings out the front door. I want to give them the best possible life. How can I give my cats an outdoor space that is safe and affordable?

One of my favorite new words in recent years is *catification*, a term created by my cat champion friends Jackson Galaxy and Kate Benjamin. Jackson hosts the popular show *My Cat from Hell* on Animal Planet and Kate is a cat-style expert and founder of Hauspanther, a site that offers feline furnishings. Catification is the art and science of designing the perfect environment to accommodate your indoor cat's needs as well as your own.

One of the most important gifts you can give your kitty duo is a safe, comforting, and engaging environment. High-quality food and ideal litter boxes are important, of course, as are cat trees, sturdy shelves, and comfy window perches—all part of this catification movement that most cats will embrace. You can step it up a notch by adding a *catio* (think "patio" with a *c*). A catio is an enclosed outdoor space that expands your cats' territory and provides them with safe access to the fresh smells, sunshine, and activities in your yard.

A catio can be a small window box enclosure, a larger three-sided structure that attaches to the side of your house, or a freestanding one in your backyard. Fully enclosed patios, decks, and porches can offer plenty of room for your cats, family, and guests.

If you are handy with a drill and hammer, you can get a DIY catio kit and build it yourself. I am not so handy. We recently hired our favorite contractor to expand our outdoor deck, add a roof, and enclose it with screens. We added a three-tiered cat tree, a large orthopedic bed for our dogs, and comfortable chairs so we can all hang out and watch the wall-mounted TV together. It was far more affordable than I expected. Of course, because the dogs share the space, we call it the *petio*.

Whatever home improvements you make for your cats' sake, please use nontoxic materials and make sure that all structures are sturdy, well built, and properly installed so that you don't have to worry about cats escaping through a gap or a torn screen. Many cats will readily take to a catio that is attached to the house through a window or other opening, but you might have to introduce them to a freestanding structure slowly, starting with short sessions to let them get used to the new space. Carry them back and forth in a closed carrier to prevent escapes and only release them when you are fully inside the structure. Pay attention to body language for signs that the great outdoors might be too overwhelming at first. Never leave cats unsupervised in a freestanding catio. 🐾

HELP FOR MY CLINIC-HATING CAT

I absolutely dread having to take my cat for his regular veterinary visits. Even when I don't do anything out of the ordinary, Oscar seems to sense when I am about to take him to the veterinary clinic and he hides under the bed. He often scratches me as I fight to pull him out. He howls all the way to the clinic, and once there, he turns into Evil Kitty. It is quite difficult for my veterinarian to examine him. Oscar is a very healthy cat who lives inside. Can I just skip these visits? It seems more like torture than it's worth.

Most cats are not fans of the three Cs: car, carrier, and clinic. Oscar definitely does not put any of these on his top 10 list of feline favorites. Even though you think you are not doing anything to tip him off, Oscar is tapping in to changes in your body chemicals (you are more anxious) and body language (your muscles are more tense). That's all he needs to initiate the under-the-bed dash.

Some cats do well when they are cared for by veterinarians with feline-only practices, because there are none of those dreaded d-o-g-s hanging out in the lobby. But cats like Oscar would fare even better if they could be seen in their homes. By examining frightened, fearfully aggressive, and people-phobic cats on their own turf, visiting veterinarians are able to obtain more accurate health readings on their patients. For example, some cats display artificially elevated blood glucose levels and blood pressure values due to stress when examined at a clinic. House-call veterinarians can also gather more clues about a cat's

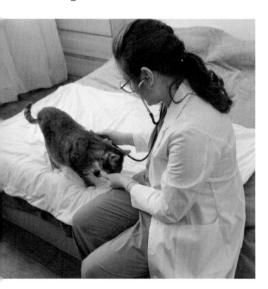

environment that may help in treating medical conditions. They get to see where the litter boxes are located and to witness the interactions of the cat with other family pets.

House-call veterinarians make sense for people who have three or more cats; forget about trying to bring that many cats all at once to the clinic. You run the risk of one escaping or testing your sanity far more than it deserves. With a house call, you receive one-stop care instead of having to book multiple appointments.

Visiting veterinarians are also the answer for people with busy schedules who have difficulty squeezing their cat's appointment in between their children's soccer and band practices, as well as those who can't drive or have medical conditions of their own. And of course, house calls are ideal for celebrities who prefer not to be mobbed by autograph hounds at a veterinary clinic.

So save your arm from scratches and keep Oscar's stress level from escalating by booking an appointment with a house-call veterinarian. House-call fees vary by location and may not be as steep as you may imagine.

And I encourage you to "sniff around" the Fear Free Happy Homes website. Fear Free is a growing movement launched by Dr. Marty Becker to offer specific tips and techniques for pet parents and pet professionals to reduce fear, anxiety, and stress in dogs and cats. The site offers lots of great articles, short videos, and downloadable graphics. I am a Fear Free pet professional, and these techniques have been positive and effective for my senior cat, Mikey, who now likes napping in his carrier and has transformed from a don't-touch-me-kitty at the veterinary clinic to happy-to-see-the-veterinarian cat. 🐾

KITTY IN THE CAR

My cat, Phil, seems to enjoy traveling in the car. Sometimes on long trips, we let him out of his carrier so he can look out the window or jump onto the back window shelf for a nap. Stuffing him into his carrier is a hassle. He sticks out his legs and arches his back when I try to push him through the opening, and he yowls when I'm carrying him.

Once he's in the car, he settles down. I know Phil is probably safer inside a carrier, but he's such a good passenger, I hate to subject him to it. Does it really matter?

Paws up for recognizing the safety importance of transporting Phil in a carrier. While it is important for cats to have freedom to prowl around inside their homes, they need to be contained inside a moving vehicle. Allowing a cat to roam freely around your vehicle can result in a *cat-astrophe*. You risk getting into an accident resulting in injury to you, your cat, and other motorists.

Your cat should never travel on your lap or in the passenger seat next to you. Here are three big reasons why.

- In an accident, an unrestrained cat becomes a projectile that could injure you or a passenger, not to mention the risk of serious injury to the cat. Even a small animal can generate more than 1,000 pounds of force upon impact in a collision at speeds as low as 35 miles per hour.

- A curious or frightened cat might slither under the driver's feet and interfere with the operation of the vehicle, or even get stuck under the gas or brake pedals. Or he could climb into the windshield and block your view or distract you.

- You may be tempted to check on your wandering feline or to give him a quick pet. Taking your eyes off the road for even a few seconds can put you in peril while driving.

The safest spot in the car for Phil is inside his carrier on the floor behind the front passenger seat. Move the seat forward to create more space for the carrier. The second-best place is the backseat with the seatbelt going through the carrier's handle and snapped into place to keep it from moving.

If Phil is fully trained to wear a properly fitted harness (see Walk This Way, page 191), another option is to let him travel in the backseat with a short leash attached to the harness and tethered firmly to a safety belt that is fastened across the seat. Make sure he can't get into the front seats and provide him with a bed to curl up in. Only do this if you are sure your cat won't try to wiggle out of the harness. You should still have a carrier in the car with you in case you make an emergency stop.

As for putting a cat into a carrier, the best way is to start with a model that has a door on the top. These have a larger and more welcoming opening that makes it easy to lower the cat in rather than pushing him through a smaller door at the front. I suggest wrapping him in a towel first, then gently setting him in the crate, towel and all.

When carrying your cat, pretend the crate handle does not exist. Grabbing a pet carrier by the handle causes a lot of rocking and motion, making some cats upset or even a little motion sick. Instead, hold the carrier with both hands like you are hugging it. You will then be able to treat Phil to a smooth, steady ride to your vehicle.

Wishing you and Phil many happy and safe road trips! 🐾

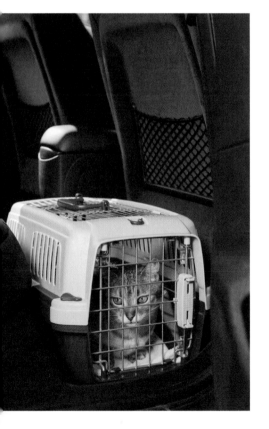

PILLOW-HOGGING PUSS

My kitty, Bebe, is adventurous and adoring by day, but turns into a pillow pig at night. At bedtime, she starts out at the foot of my bed while I brush my teeth. When I crawl under the covers, she creeps forward and nestles by my side. But by the middle of the night when I am in a deep sleep, she has commandeered my pillow. She walks right over me and wakes me up. I like having her sleep on my bed, but how can I keep her off my pillow so I can get some sleep?

When it comes to sharing your bed with your cat, you're not alone. About 50 percent of cat parents welcome their cats to sleep with them at night. And why not? Those furry bodies and soothing purrs may lull you to sleep and help calm nighttime anxieties. A study conducted at the Mayo Clinic Sleep Disorders Center, however, found that about half of the people who let pets share their bed at night suffer from disrupted sleep that results in their being tired each morning. The researchers also found that many people are so attached to their pets that they are willing to tolerate poor sleep in order to be near them at night.

I admit that my bed is often full of pets, including my little dog, Emma. Fortunately, I'm a heavy sleeper and my cats prefer to carve out spots on the bed by my legs or at the bottom of the bed. In your case, however, Bebe sounds like one bossy cat. She feels entitled to sleep wherever she chooses, regardless of your preferences. Cute as she may be, you need to regain control of your bed and your pillow and to reinstate some bed boundaries. Start by making the bottom of your bed more appealing. Provide Bebe with her own plush pillow or soft fleecy blanket. Praise her when she settles down there. Be consistent about moving her to the bottom of your bed before you

are asleep. Or compromise by providing Bebe with her own pillow next to yours.

To make your territory less appealing, consider lightly spraying your pillow with a citrus scent (one you enjoy). Cats are not fond of that aroma. If she wakes you up in the middle of the night, either put her back in her spot or push her to the floor. After being ousted a few times, most cats get the idea and adjust to the new bedroom rules.

You may sacrifice a few nights of sleep to teach Bebe about the new no-pillow zone, but she will soon realize she has a great spot at the foot of your bed. Sweet dreams! 🐾

AAH, THE GREAT INDOORS

My cat, Bruno, is a big, muscular cat. He is very friendly and easygoing. Since he was a kitten, he has ventured wherever he pleases around the neighborhood. Our property is one acre with some woods. Bruno is now 10 years old and seems to be slowing down a bit. Our winters here are cold and nasty. The addition of a recent housing development in our neighborhood has created more traffic on our street. For all these reasons, I'd like Bruno to become an indoor cat. What's the best way for me to do this without upsetting him?

I can tell you have already assessed the "feline fear factor." You recognize that Bruno's age plus worsening weather and increasing traffic pose a greater chance of his becoming injured or ill due to his free-roaming lifestyle. With Bruno indoors, you will no longer have to worry about him developing an abscess from scrapping with a stray, risking exposure to poisonous yard-care products or antifreeze, or contracting a contagious disease like feline leukemia.

It's only natural to feel a little guilt at first. You are probably assuming that Bruno will feel that his freedom has been yanked from him. He may indeed act out in undesirable ways: urine marking, yowling at the door, or clawing your sofa. Remind yourself that your actions stem from genuine love and concern for Bruno. You are giving Bruno the best gift you can give him—a longer, healthier life.

To avoid bad behaviors, you need to make his indoor domain far more stimulating and appealing than the outside scene that he is used to. An outdoor cat exercises more and engages his senses more, so you will need to replace the sights, smells, and sounds of the outdoors. Bruno may be 10 years old, but he probably has a lot of kittenish play left in him. He needs daily exercise and interactive play sessions to keep him happy and not pining for the outdoor life. Catnip mice, cat wands, and feather toys on sticks can all be used to bring out the playful predator in Bruno and to give him appropriate outlets for hunting, stalking, and chasing. Look for toys that he can play with by himself, such as a ball in a round track or a mouse on an elastic string that you hang in a

doorway. Put some kibble in a hollow toy that he can bat around to make the treats trickle out.

Provide Bruno with suitable places to scratch and claw and a comfy perch where he can view what's happening outside. Position sturdy scratching posts in key rooms where the two of you spend a lot of time, such as the living room and bedroom. Install a window perch that overlooks a bird feeder or a tree where the local squirrel gang likes to hang out.

If you have the room and the budget, consider adding a catio that will allow Bruno to safely enjoy the outdoors. (See Give Me a C for Catio, page 178.)

Indoors Is Best

Indoor cats live longer than their outdoor counterparts. Statistics from the Humane Society of the United States show that outdoor cats, on average, live to age 5. Indoor cats, however, can live into their late teens, even early 20s. While many outdoor cats do live long and healthy lives, they are exposed to many more dangers. Outdoor cats face increased risk of injury and illness. Many meet an untimely end under the wheels of a car or from an animal attack.

Learn more about making your feline a happy homebody by visiting the websites of the Indoor Pet Initiative, sponsored by The Ohio State University College of Veterinary Medicine, or Cat Friendly Homes, sponsored by the American Association of Feline Practitioners (see Useful Websites, page 216).

Bruno may protest his new confinement. If he starts making loud demands at the door, your natural instinct may be to yell at him to quiet down. That won't work. You two will only get in a "who can yell louder" match. And guess what? You'll lose. Instead, ignore him. It won't be easy initially and your patience will be tested. When he is quiet for even a few seconds, call him over to give him a treat or scratch his chin or play a game with him. In time, his yowling will subside as he realizes you are not caving in to his demands.

Inappropriate elimination can be a problem for a cat making the transition to indoor life. If Bruno has traditionally performed his bathroom duties outside, you may need to teach him how to use a litter box. I recommend you confine Bruno to a small but cozy room for a week or so. Provide him with a litter box that you scoop out daily. Locate his bed and his food and water bowls on the opposite side of the room from the box. Ideally, this room should have a window where he can look out. Provide Bruno with a window perch. Consider playing music on low volume and spend some time playing and cuddling with him each day. Make sure he has plenty of toys to amuse himself.

You can't tone down Mother Nature and you usually can't stop progress, but you can take the necessary steps in your own home to make it feel feline friendly to Bruno. 🐾

CAN MY CAT BE A THERAPY CAT?

Now that I'm retired from teaching, I want to do more volunteering, especially at senior centers. My 2-year-old cat, Finn, is Mr. Social. He loves meeting people and is very smart. Nothing seems to really rattle him. He doesn't mind traveling in the car and seems eager to learn new things. Does he have what it takes to be a therapy cat?

Dogs make up the majority of certified therapy animals, but the number of therapy cats is increasing. Felines are small, easy to pick up, and possess one major advantage over dogs: the soothing sound of purring. Not every cat was born to be a therapy cat, but those who are provide a healing "fur fix" to people in hospitals and nursing homes, and to homebound seniors as well as to kids at camps and schools.

My orange tabby, Casey, is a certified therapy cat. He is easygoing, loves learning new tricks, and purrs all the time. He also seems to enjoy sporting a cowboy hat and riding in his pet stroller when we make regular visits to see residents at a memory care center in Dallas. I often say that Casey has never met a stranger or been in a strange place. He adapts quickly to people and to situations—essential qualities in a therapy cat.

Finn's easygoing style and desire to greet people are two key traits necessary for therapy cats. That he doesn't mind car travel is a plus, as most cats prefer to be homebodies and don't like adjusting to new surroundings. Make sure he is

fine about having his paw pads gently pressed and all parts of his body being touched. See how he reacts when other people handle him.

Contact a therapy animal organization such as Love on a Leash or Pet Partners to find a certification program in your area. Although each program differs, the ground rules call for cats to be at least 1 year old; fully updated on all their vaccinations; in good health; and able to tolerate travel, loud noises, crowds, strange smells, and frequent handling. They must be good-natured about being poked at or pulled on, and be comfortable with people of all ages.

As part of your training, you and Finn will make supervised visits to be sure he has the right therapy skills and that you make a good team. These organizations offer their teams comprehensive insurance coverage while on volunteer visits, assistance finding places to visit, and photo ID badges to wear while visiting.

To ensure Finn's safety, I recommend you train him to wear a harness and walk on a leash. He will definitely win admiration if he can strut into a room on a leash, but it's a good idea for him to be comfortable riding in a pet stroller, too. Cats able to perform tricks such as paw waving, sitting up on their hind legs, and jumping into open arms on cue will make a great impression as well. Of course, possessing a strong, steady purr only enhances his popularity among people in need of a little TLC (tender loving cat).

It sounds like Finn checks all the right boxes. I can tell you from personal experience with Casey that this is a great way to give back to your community and to give your cat a full and enriched life. 🐾

AM I TOO OLD TO ADOPT A CAT?

After 10 years of retirement, I found my large home to be too big and too time consuming to maintain. I recently moved to a nice assisted-living center in my community. One selling point was that residents are allowed to have small pets. I'm thinking about adopting a kitten or cat from my local shelter but wonder if I am too old to adopt. Any advice?

Never underestimate the power of pets to improve people's lives, no matter what their age or living situation. More and more senior living centers recognize the many benefits of living with companion animals. Especially for people who live alone, pets offer affection, warmth, and companionship, and promote a sense of responsibility and routine.

I encourage you to meet with adoption staff at your local animal center. They will work with you to match a feline that is compatible with your personality and your living arrangements. Take your time making your selection. Offer to foster at first to make sure you and the cat are well suited.

Here are a couple of things to think about: Kittens are cute, but they are also full of energy and mischief. They might scratch or bite in play and will almost certainly romp around at night for the first year or so. Consider adopting an older cat whose personality is established. Senior cats in need of rescuing are usually very appreciative of finding a "retirement" home of their own. You might also think about doubling the fun with two cats, especially if you find a bonded pair who already have a relationship.

Keep in mind that you will be responsible for keeping your new cat up to date on necessary vaccinations and veterinary care, not to mention cleaning the litter box regularly. And you must take care that your cat does not dash out the door and run loose down the hallway or into a communal area. But the benefits are countless. Your fun, furry roommate is sure to be good company and may be the spark for you to meet other pet lovers in your center. 🐾

TAKE A HIKE, KITTY

I think my cat, Billy, is a dog who purrs! He walks on a leash and harness, loves riding in his carrier, and seems to want to go with me when I head to the front door. What can I do to safely bring him on more outdoor adventures?

Ah, it is a great time to be a cool, confident, smart cat like Billy. He lives during the Age of Adventure Cats! More people all over the world are taking hikes, going kayaking or sailing, and having other outdoor adventures with their felines. Well-tempered, confident cats can accompany their favorite people to pet-welcoming outdoor cafés, overnight visits to family and friends, and much more. Emily Hall is the founder of KittyCatGO, a group for people with cats who love to travel. She believes, as do I, that enriching your cat's life with adventure, big or small, will help to give your cat a more fulfilled life.

Hall identifies six personality traits of a feline adventurer and suggests you determine your cat's likes and dislikes. Her cat Sophie enjoys group hikes, even with dogs, because she is very outgoing and social. But her other cat, Kylo Ren, prefers one-on-one hikes with Hall, far from crowds.

- Sociable/friendly
- Easily handled
- Confident/not easily spooked
- Inquisitive/engaged
- High energy
- Food motivated

Is Billy an adventure cat? It sounds like he is ready to expand his horizons, as he is happy on your neighborhood walks. For safety, make sure he wears a comfortable, properly fitted harness with a leash connected to the D ring. Gradually expose him to new places with new distractions, always paying attention to his reactions. Keep your outings brief at first. If he isn't used to dogs, I recommend that you avoid walks during peak dog walking times—typically, early morning and early evening. But have a game plan for encountering them—many places and activities that welcome adventure cats also attract dog owners!

Because he is already comfortable with a harness and leash, I suggest you also accustom Billy to a backpack carrier made especially for cats. They feature breathable material, a viewing window, and a safety tether for attaching his harness. On longer walks or overnight adventures, they provide a safe, comfortable place for your cat to rest and retreat. Pack bottled water and a collapsible bowl, but don't be surprised if Billy doesn't lap up water during breaks like dogs do. To keep him hydrated on hikes, bring lickable treats to provide fluids on the go. Popular versions made by Hartz, Friskies, Tiki Cats, and others are available at pet supply stores and online.

And of course, before you leave home, always make sure Billy is wearing a collar with ID. If he isn't already microchipped, make an appointment with your veterinarian. 🐾

WALK THIS WAY

My cat, Sissy, is quite curious and very mellow. I just moved into a quiet neighborhood after living in an apartment for a couple of years. I would like to take her for walks to give her a chance to be outside. How can I train her to tolerate a harness and leash?

Your success in training your cat to walk on a leash and harness outside depends first on your attitude. Trust me, cats can read our bluffs. If you're apprehensive or unsure about the process or become impatient, your cat will read that message loud and clear.

Second, heed this cardinal cat rule: When it comes to sauntering outside on a tether, cats call the shots. Don't expect Sissy to start heeling like a poodle who just graduated top in her obedience training class. Sissy leads and you follow.

Third, never attempt to take Sissy on a walk with only a leash. You need to fit Sissy with a harness so there is no chance that she could become spooked and slip out of a collar and get lost. Do not use a small dog harness. You need one designed for cats so there

is no chance for her to squirm out. Fortunately, there are many good-quality cat harnesses now available.

Harness training is best accomplished in the following stages:

1. When you bring home the harness and leash, leave them next to Sissy's food bowl or scratching post for a few days. Say nothing. Let her approach on her own to check them out.

2. When Sissy is in a relaxed, contented mood, engage her in a little play with the harness and leash. Dangle the harness and let her swat at it. Drag the leash on the floor to entice her to chase and pounce on it. You are associating these training tools with fun and games in your cat's mind.

3. Next, put the harness on Sissy inside your house and offer lots of praise and a couple of treats. Let her walk around freely wearing it. Not all cats are fans of harnesses, and you have to respect their personal preferences. If she struggles or tries to rub the harness off, calmly remove it and repeat step 2 before trying again. But if she seems okay, let her wear the harness for a few minutes and then take it off.

4. It's time to attach the leash to your harness-wearing cat. Again, keep this stage indoors and monitor Sissy's level of acceptance. Initially, do not hold the leash to allow Sissy to adjust to the feel of the leash as she moves. After she becomes accustomed to dragging it behind her, pick it up and let her lead you around.

5. Once she has accepted walking around the house wearing a harness, you're ready to head outdoors. Limit your first

outing to a safe haven such as your backyard or front porch and encourage her to sniff around and decide what direction to take. Remember, the goal is to build slowly on each success.

6. After a few days, you should be ready to head down your driveway and possibly a bit down the sidewalk. Pick quiet times in your neighborhood to limit possible distractions.

You want to make this a pleasant experience. Unless you have that rare cat who is eager to go for a long walk, keep your excursions short. If you live on a busy street, put your cat in a cat stroller or a cat backpack and head for a quiet place like a park where she may feel more secure. Again, remember to first introduce a cat stroller or backpack inside the safe confines of your home to test your cat's receptiveness to these items before heading outside.

My cats, Casey and Rusty, are proud harness-wearing, leash-walking felines. They also dig riding tethered inside a pet stroller. Remember to keep Sissy's preferences in mind. With dogs, it is all about distance, but cats often prefer a short stroll with stops to smell flowers, flop and roll on the sun-kissed sidewalk, and nibble on a few blades of grass. You may not travel far, but your brief jaunts will offer Sissy plenty of adventure. 🐾

DASHING OUT THE DOOR

Whenever I leave or enter the house through the door leading to the garage, my big orange tabby, Morris, stands ready to bolt out the door. He is a muscular, pushy cat. Sometimes I can't reach the garage door opener quickly enough to shut the overhead garage door before Morris scoots out and down the driveway. He's supposed to be an indoor cat, so I have to run after him and bring him home, which can take a long time. What can I do to keep Morris from bolting out the door?

What makes an indoor cat feel the need to prowl outside? Morris may be smelling and hearing other cats, especially during the breeding seasons, or he may be curious about the trees and grass he can see from the window (not to mention the birds!). He obviously hates to be a homebody. He doesn't understand that he is safer inside. He also thinks he can push his weight around with you.

You can retrain Morris to meet and greet you at a particular spot when you leave or return home. Practice luring Morris over to a favorite place, such as a window perch or a cat tree. Then say your goodbyes there. Give him a special treat or a pinch of catnip to occupy him while you exit.

If he likes to chase things, take a paper wad, crinkle it in your hand to make enticing sounds, and toss it in the opposite direction as you exit. Or toss him a toy mouse to distract him. Also, randomly choose different doors to enter and leave. A cat can't lie in wait at three different exits. Practice with the

193

main garage door shut, so that even if Morris turns into Houdini, you'll be able to recapture him easily.

When you come home, make sure that the garage door is closed while you practice your returns. Walk in the house door, completely ignoring the ever-waiting Morris. Go over to the chosen spot. Call him over, greet him, and offer him a treat. The idea is to motivate Morris to move away from the door when you leave and when you come home in exchange for a tasty payoff at the window perch or cat tree.

Another method is to discourage him from approaching the door at all. One of my friends had a similar problem with her bolting cat. She placed squirt guns on either side of the exit door. When she was coming or going, she aimed low and squirted her cat in the chest area. It caught him off guard enough to cause him not to stand so close to the door anymore. Just take careful aim and do not splash Morris in the face. A noisy shaker (you can make one by dropping a few pennies in an empty beverage can and taping the opening shut) or a few sharp claps of your hand might chase him away long enough for you to get through the door safely.

Consider satisfying your cat's need to experience the outdoors by installing a window enclosure or taking him for walks. Fit him in a harness attached to a leash and let him sniff and scout out what's happening on your block. Many cats can become accustomed to wearing a leash if you take it slowly and reward him for small steps (see Walk This Way, page 191).

If Morris does escape, please don't scold him or reprimand him when he returns to the house. You will only confuse him and possibly dampen his desire to come home. 🐾

POOF! DISAPPEARING CAT!

Recently, my neighbor's Japanese Bobtail became lost when a repairman left the back door open. We organized a neighborhood search for Jinx, and fortunately, we found him the next day hiding in shrubbery about three houses away. As an owner of two indoor cats, I worry what would happen if they should suddenly find themselves outside. Why would contented indoor cats want to venture outside on their own? What tips can you offer to do a thorough job of trying to find them?

All of us with indoor cats feel a bit nervous when we think about the possibility of our pampered pets facing the dangers of the outside world. Even contented feline homebodies possess natural hunting instincts and curiosity.

The sights, sounds, and smells of the outdoors can prove to be far more alluring than simply sunning on the sofa. Cats think in the present. A door opens and the cat slips out. He doesn't make contingency plans for what happens if he forgets his way home. But we can better the chances of finding our cats if we recognize typical lost-cat behaviors.

Most indoor cats who slip out a door do not venture very far. Indoor cats tend to hide rather than flee because hiding is an instinctive response. That said,

they can be darn good at hiding and extremely challenging to coax out of hard-to-reach spots.

Know your cat's personality. That's important because it will aid in finding him. You may be interested to learn that cats fall into four general personality types. Let me share with you the best game for finding each of these types.

Xenophobic cats are scared of anything new or the unknown. They tend to dash and hide when guests come into your home and refuse to resurface until hours after the guests depart. If they find themselves outside, these cats tend to freeze out of fear and do not go far. If you have such a cat who gets lost, the best plan is to set a baited humane trap

195

near your home. Place a dish of tuna inside to lure your cat into the trap.

Cautious cats initially disappear when guests come to your home, but then slowly enter the room to check out the newcomers. If your cat fits this description, the plan should be to conduct a thorough search of surrounding homes and to set baited humane traps in your neighbors' yards. These cats, once they muster the courage, tend to come out of hiding after a day or so and try to retrace their steps back home. They may even meow while hiding if they hear your voice.

Aloof cats will avoid people they don't know, including members of a search-and-rescue group. This type will eventually come out of hiding and either show up meowing at your door or start to travel. For these cats, the best plan is to set up baited humane traps throughout the neighborhood, while searching yards and other areas near where they escaped.

Outgoing, curious cats act like the ambassador to your home. They enjoy meeting and greeting your guests. If you have a cat that matches this description, be aware that he is likely to wander as he is not easily frightened. The best game plan with this type involves speaking with neighbors, because your cat may have charmed one of them into bringing him inside and feeding him.

When searching for your cat, resist running, because swift movement might frighten him and cause him to go into deeper hiding. Websites such as Nextdoor are effective in posting about your cat's disappearance. If you have a neighborhood listserv or Facebook page, use it. Be sure to include your cat's photo and to describe his personality.

If you happen to have more than one indoor cat and they get along very well, consider putting the feline pal inside a carrier and taking her with you when you search the area. The scent of this cat may be enough to lure your lost cat out of hiding.

For any lost cat, post brightly colored posters within a radius of several blocks. Make the posters eye-catching and include a photo of your cat, his name, your contact info, and perhaps a reward. And don't forget other avenues such as contacting regional veterinary clinics, local shelters, animal control, and police departments in your locale.

One final strategy: If possible, leave a sliding door open 4 to 6 inches or a back door or garage door propped open a bit. Some cats wait until dark to come out of hiding and may come back home when they feel it is safe to do so. You may be relieved in the morning at the sight of your "lost" cat sitting next to her bowl waiting for breakfast. 🐾

Meet Kim Freeman, Cat Detective

Kim Freeman is the Sherlock Holmes of finding lost cats. As founder of Lost Cat Finder, Freeman is recognized as the world's first full-time cat detective. She often teams up with her purring partner, Henry, to find missing cats all over the United States as well as in 16 other countries.

Freeman tracks down missing cats and never relies on a search-and-rescue dog to aid her because most cats do not want to be found by a dog, even a trained professional one. Her clicker-trained, harnessed Henry is scent-focused to find felines. He sports a lighted cat collar with a small camera so Freeman can keep up with Henry's search in the dark and see what he sees.

Freeman offers these insights into finding lost cats:

- Look closely near your home. Dogs roam, cats hide. People tend to look all over town for their cat, but they really need to comb areas within their neighborhood.

- Don't try to lure your cat back home by putting his litter box on the front porch. This strategy can backfire. The scent of the litter may attract wildlife, perhaps even predators like foxes, or a territorial neighborhood cat who may chase your cat farther away.

- Resist walking around and calling for your cat by name and shaking a container of treats. Your cat may move toward your voice but may be still too scared to come out of hiding and may end up farther from home.

- Do not chase your cat. They are too fast. Even a three-legged cat can outrun a person. Chasing will make your cat feel like prey and he may run farther and faster. Instead, sit down on your front porch or another place on your property. Open a can of tuna to get your cat to come to you.

I also advocate training your cat to come to a whistle. It is a distinctive sound. Start training indoors and offer your cat a treat or two when he comes trotting your way at the sound of the whistle. I have whistled-trained all my cats (and now my dogs also race my way when they hear the tweet sound).

It paid off when Rusty, my young ginger cat, slipped out the back door. I didn't panic. I whistled. He turned around as I said, "Want a treat, Rusty? Let's come back inside." He happily followed me indoors, where he collected his treats. Whew!

LET'S SEE SOME ID

My indoor cat, Chance, wears an identification tag on his collar. He never seems to want to go outside. My beagle, on the other hand doesn't always come when he is called. I spent the money on a microchip ID for the dog, but I don't see the need to do the same for Chance. Am I wrong?

Even though Chance loves the indoor life, he could find himself lost. We can't control our cats' movements every moment. He may become lost during a car trip, if a door is left open in your home, or under other circumstances.

The cost of microchipping is quite affordable these days and is totally priceless when it comes to reuniting lost pets with their grateful owners. Contact your veterinarian or local animal shelter to find out more about the procedure. Many clinics and shelters offer discount microchipping on certain days of the month or during a special event.

Even though Chance sports an ID tag, he could lose his collar. That's why I'm a big promoter of having pets microchipped. Microchipping does not automatically guarantee the safe return of your lost cat, but it sure increases the odds.

Microchipping is a quick and virtually painless procedure. Your cat does not need to be anesthetized. A veterinarian uses a special needle to insert the microchip (about the size of a grain of rice) under your cat's skin between the shoulder blades. A cat found with no outward signs of identification can be scanned for the presence of a microchip using a special wand device commonly found in animal shelters and veterinary clinics. The microchip provides your contact information as well as your veterinary clinic and the manufacturer of the chip.

Sadly, about 40 percent of people who microchip their pets fail to take the final processing step. The chip is useless if it does not contain your contact info. Make sure you fill out the enrollment paperwork and mail it in (with a nominal, one-time fee) to the manufacturer of the chip or a national recovery service. Enrollment should be kept up to date if you move, and having a service that is available 7 days a week/24 hours a day is the best protection. 🐾

YIKES! WE'RE MOVING!

I am moving to a new apartment in six months with Misha, my 11-year-old cat. I am wondering what I should be doing to make this move less stressful for her. She has had a history of urinary tract problems—all solved—and with that came a habit of overgrooming to the point of pulling out her hair. She is alone all day, but I do play with her at night. I would say she's a bit high-strung. Any advice on how to make this move go smoothly for her?

Moving is stressful for everyone, but cats in particular detest breaks in their routines. The sight of furniture being moved, items being packed, and strange people coming in and out of their feline "castle" can take a toll on their self-confidence and trigger some unwanted behaviors (like hiding, not eating, or inappropriate urination).

Cats are also territorial. They don't like to vacate their home turfs, and in an unfamiliar place, they feel insecure and stressed by new sounds, smells, and the urge to find safety zones.

You mention that Misha is a bit high-strung. Because moving takes a toll on all members of the household, you will be feeling the stress as well, and

she will detect signs of your tension. If you are uptight, she may surmise that something is terribly wrong.

Fortunately, you can do a lot to prepare Misha for your move and the new apartment. The most important step is to introduce her to feeling safe inside a carrier long before moving day. Start by leaving the carrier where Misha likes to catnap. Make it tempting by placing a comfy blanket inside and leaving the door open. Sprinkle some catnip inside if she likes the scent. You are helping her create good associations with the carrier.

Once Misha seems comfortable in the carrier, shut her in it and take her out to your car. Just hang out with her for a few minutes without turning on the ignition. Gradually work up to taking her on short car rides.

As moving day approaches, try to stick to as regular a routine as possible. Strange as it sounds, tell Misha about the move and what is happening. Use an upbeat, positive tone. True, she won't know your words, but she will read your mood and posture. Let her sniff and explore packing boxes, tape, and other moving supplies.

I recommend that both you and Misha take a calming herbal blend called Rescue Remedy. This over-the-counter blend of essential botanical oils is available at pet supply stores and health stores. It is not toxic or addictive. Place a dropperful in a glass of water for you and rub a few drops into the tips of Misha's ears (it enters her body through the tiny capillaries in the ears). Some cats may require a calming prescriptive medicine—check with your veterinarian.

On moving day, put a T-shirt that you've worn but haven't washed in Misha's carrier. Having your familiar scent nearby may help reassure her and keep her calm. At the new location, keep Misha in her carrier in a bathroom or large closet and post a big sign alerting the movers not to open the door, because there is a cat inside. Even better, sign her up to spend the day at a cat-friendly boarding facility or at a friend's house where she can have a room to herself without the strange sounds and distraction of the movers.

As you settle into your new place, keep Misha confined in one room with all her amenities (food and water bowls, litter box, bedding, toys), making sure to separate the dishes and the litter box as much as possible. Leave her carrier with her so she can hide in it if she wants. Maybe play a little music to muffle the sounds of unpacking. Let her become comfortable exploring this room for a day or so before you introduce her to other rooms in the apartment.

These strategies help all cats, including high-strung ones like Misha, feel right at home in their new places. Good luck! 🐾

KITTY WANTS ROOM SERVICE

I plan to take a long road trip to visit my favorite aunt this summer. She loves my cat, Tommy, a lot and insists he come for the visit. I expect I will need to book a couple of nights in hotels each way to reach my aunt's house. How can I make the hotel visit fun and, more important, safe for Tommy?

I've traveled to many hotels across the country with as many as three cats in tow. Casey, my ginger boy who assists me in my pet first aid and pet behavior talks, has traveled by plane and car to 13 states and counting. He has proven to be a great travel mate and four-legged hotel guest.

With a little planning, you can ensure the hotel stays are welcoming to you and Tommy. First, hit the internet before you hit the road. Head to pet travel websites to find hotels that welcome pets. Read the reviews from other pet travelers. Book the hotels in advance—don't try to walk in and hope to find an available room. You are traveling many miles and having hotel reservations gives you peace of mind at the end of a long day behind the wheel.

If available, ask for a wheelchair-accessible room. The reason? The bathrooms tend to be more spacious, making them the best place for a traveling cat to hang out and reducing the risk of him escaping down the hallway.

201

Research pet resources near the hotel. Before you book, look online for the nearest emergency and regular veterinary clinic. In case of an emergency, when every minute might count, you don't want to waste time locating a clinic. Upload a copy of his medical records to your phone and keep a printed version in an envelope tucked into the carrier or zipped into a side pocket. You may need to show these records at check-in, depending on the hotel's pet policy.

Bring a portable litter box that you can place in the bathroom. Consider the disposable ones that come packed with litter. Or get lightweight litter and one or two easy-to-clean foldable litter boxes made of washable canvas (available online). Don't forget to bring a scoop and plenty of bags.

Bring plenty of Tommy's usual food, canned or dry. Do not switch diets on the road as cats have sensitive digestive systems and the added stress from the travel could cause gastrointestinal issues, such as vomiting or diarrhea, if a new food is introduced. Bring bottled water to reduce the risk of him getting an upset stomach from drinking water from a faucet. Bring his bedding and a favorite toy to add to his comfort and to engage him in purposeful play once he has thoroughly checked out the nooks and crannies of the hotel room.

Practice feline travel safety. Tommy should wear a harness, ideally one with an identification tag hooked on to the D ring. Breakaway collars earn their names for a reason: They are designed to release when pulled to prevent neck injuries to the cat. The harness option ensures Tommy always wears his ID.

Before you let Tommy out of the carrier, do a thorough inspection of the room. To prevent him from squeezing into a tight spot or disappearing under the bed, block his access with objects such as spare pillows and suitcases. Close the closet door and put down the toilet lid. Most important tip: Hang a Do Not Disturb sign on the doorknob to prevent an unexpected visit by the housekeeping staff. You do not want a frightened or curious Tommy to slip out a door left ajar.

During your travels, try to stay calm and upbeat. Cats can read our emotions. Avoid making loud noises or exaggerated gestures that may startle or stress Tommy while traveling and in the hotel room.

Finally, practice pawing it forward. Traveling with a pet and staying in a nice hotel is a privilege, not a right. So be sure to alert the staff you have a cat in your room and tip generously to encourage the hotel management to maintain its pet-friendly policy. 🐾

Traveling Cat Checklist

Before you hit the road with your cat, stock your car with supplies.

- A well-ventilated cat carrier with an easy-to-clean floor pad
- Bottled water and a no-spill bowl
- A supply of your cat's usual food, small bowl, and treats
- Favorite toys
- Comfy, familiar blanket
- An extra leash and harness, in case you lose one
- A spare collar and ID tags

- Pet first-aid kit
- Travel litter box, litter, scoop, and bags for waste
- Roll of paper towels and enzyme-based stain-and-odor spray
- Nonprescription calming medicine such as Rescue Remedy or Feliway
- Photo of your cat in case he gets lost
- Your cat's medical records

TO BOARD OR NOT TO BOARD

We're planning a three-week European vacation next summer with our entire family. We all are excited about this trip, but we are debating whether to board our two cats or to hire a pet sitter to take care of them. With all of us traveling together, we don't have our normal cat sitters. Either option is expensive, but we don't want to worry about them when we're gone. Bonnie and Clyde are siblings, about 4 years old, who are very bonded with each other. They are basically indoor cats and have traveled with us for weekend visits at my parents' home without much fuss. Which option would work out best for them?

You won't find many cats packing passports. Because your cats would probably choose to stay home, the pet-sitting option is definitely worth considering. The main benefit of pet sitting is that Bonnie and Clyde are able to stay put with all their creature comforts. Even though your absence will upset their normal routine, they will be surrounded by familiar scents and will be comforted by being on their own turf.

I recommend you interview professional sitters who belong to a national organization such as Pet Sitters International or the National Association of Professional Pet Sitters. Pet sitters are trained to feed your cat, administer medications, and scoop the litter boxes. They also are available to water your plants, make sure your windows and doors are locked, take in the newspaper and mail, and even take out the trash. They are also licensed, bonded, and insured, and many of them are trained in pet first aid.

Always provide a written list of instructions on how to care for your cats and what to do in case of a medical emergency.

Now let's consider the boarding option. In addition to the traditional veterinary clinic boarding, there are increasing numbers of specialty kennels that cater to your pet's every whim. Instead of going to the dogs, these places are beginning to go to the cats. Some places look like mini-condos, complete with a television set, piped-in music, plush bedding, two levels, window perches, and other cat amenities.

If you decide to board Bonnie and Clyde, look for a cat-only kennel, especially if your cats have not had a lot of whisker-to-whisker time with

dogs. A feline environment will be more soothing to your cats, without all that barking, whining, and howling. It's important that you visit the places before booking rather than rely on information collected over the phone from the kennel staff or looking at the facility's website.

When you visit, pay attention to how the staff interacts with feline guests. You definitely want "cat people" who will cuddle and call your cats by their names. Ask what the ratio of staff to cats is, if the place is staffed 24 hours a day, and if there is a veterinarian on call to handle medical emergencies. The kennel should be clean, and you should not smell any odors. If permitted, take a careful look at the feline guests and determine if they look content or act edgy or scared. And don't forget to ask that Bonnie and Clyde share a run.

Because they are close companions, staying together will help ease the distress of being away from home.

As your trip won't occur for several months, I encourage you to take a test run by booking Bonnie and Clyde for a night or two at a kennel. If they appear totally stressed out when you pick them up, that's a sign that the kennel life, even at a fancy feline resort, is not for them.

So, what's my vote? That's a tough call. Try the boarding for a couple of days, wait a week or so, and then the next time you plan to see your folks for a weekend, leave Bonnie and Clyde with a pet sitter and see how they do. You should be able to tell from their behavior which option makes the most sense for your duo. With names like Bonnie and Clyde, you want to keep them happy! 🐾

HARASSING THE HOUSEGUESTS

My cat, Simon, is an outgoing guy who struts around as if he rules the house. Although he is neutered and well behaved (at least with me), his reactions toward houseguests vary, depending on who is visiting, how long they stay, and to what extent they disrupt his routine. Sometimes he is quite friendly, and other times he is downright mean. He even peed in my uncle's open suitcase during one long visit.

My other cat, Garfunkel, treats all houseguests the same. He runs and hides and tries to stay out of their sight. What can I do to ease Garfunkel's fears and to make Simon treat our guests with better manners?

With names like these, it's a shame there is a lack of harmony with houseguests. One of your problems may be that cats crave routines. They become accustomed to a sedate, indulged life. They usually don't enjoy surprises like the arrival of a strange-smelling person who may rudely commandeer the spare bedroom where they are accustomed to taking their afternoon naps. Too many changes, too fast, without proper planning, can trigger acute stress and unhappiness.

Even sociable cats such as Simon can get annoyed or overstimulated by houseguests. How each cat reacts depends a lot on his age, health status, temperament, personality, lifestyle, and previous experience with unfamiliar people. Some cats become upset enough to mark their territory by urinating on the belongings of guests.

One thing you can do to make visits go more smoothly is to remind your guests of all your furry roommates and to describe any particular habits. Also mention a few house rules regarding your pets.

- Don't rush up to them to greet—let them decide if they wish to approach you.

- If your cats live indoors only, be careful when opening doors.

- No sneaking them table scraps or other human food.

A few days before your guests arrive, slowly relocate your cats' bedding from the spare bedroom to a new safe haven that is off-limits to guests, such as a den or spare bathroom. Keep the door to the guest room closed and advise your guests to do the same.

When guests arrive, strive to maintain as much of a daily routine as possible for your cats. That means cleaning out the litter boxes regularly and feeding your cats at the usual time and place. Spend at least a few minutes each day playing with your cats and devoting some time for cuddling. You may consider masking loud or unfamiliar noises (like your uncle's heavy snoring or your sister's high-pitched giggles) by playing a radio or sound machine softly in your cats' safe haven space. Don't force your pets to interact with your guests.

For cats exhibiting signs of stress, you might try easing anxiety with a product called Feliway. It mimics a comforting facial pheromone produced by cats and comes as a wall plug-in. This product, available at pet supply stores, diffuses the pheromones throughout a room.

If your cat does engage in inappropriate elimination or other destructive behavior, recognize that he is signaling that he is extremely stressed and feels the need to mark his territory. Do not punish him because that can only heighten his stress. 🐾

feline fact

The phrase *the cat's pajamas* was coined by E. B. Katz, an English tailor in the late 1700s. He made silk pajamas for the British elite.

CLICK! CLICK! TRAIN YOUR TABBY

My husband and I have different views on whether cats are capable of learning tricks. My husband believes that cats are out to please only themselves and have no interest in doing some of the tricks that dogs do willingly. I believe that with the right motivation, we can train our cat to shake paws, sit up, and follow other commands. I hope you can settle this bet. Which one of us is right?

You win this bet, paws down. Cats are not commonly thought of as performers, but many do participate in circuses, street shows, and movies. One effective method for working with cats is clicker training. Clicker training involves the use of a small device that makes a distinctive sound to reinforce desired actions. Karen Pryor, a pioneering animal behaviorist, first used clicker training with dolphins at Sea World in the 1960s. Two decades later, she began employing this innovative method of positive reinforcement on dogs, cats, and other critters.

Clicker training is a positive technique that relies on operant conditioning to shape a desired action or behavior without force or cajoling. The premise is simple: Encourage the animal to perform desired actions by rewarding appropriate behavior. Clicker training works because there is no punishment involved. You draw attention to the behaviors you're seeking in your cat and ignore other actions.

As for your own cat, here are some ways you can bring out his true talents through clicker training. You can buy a small, plastic clicker at most pet supply stores, or you can use a ballpoint pen. Whichever you use, it is important that you stick with it so that its distinctive sound serves as a cue for your feline student. Make the clicking sound and then offer a small treat. In the first few sessions, you are merely introducing the clicker sound to your cat and establishing that the sound equals a treat.

Timing is key to clicker training's success. When your cat does something you want, for example raising his front paw, you need to immediately press the clicker, hand over a small treat, and say *Paw* to reinforce the desired behavior. In time, the lightbulb will turn on inside your cat's head as he starts to recognize the link between the word *Paw* and the sound of the reinforcing click.

To use a clicker to teach your cat to sit on cue, start by luring him into a sitting position with a food treat that you slowly move over his head toward his back. Let gravity be your ally. As his head follows the treat, his back end will naturally touch the floor. When this happens, click and hand over the treat. Clicking signals "mission accomplished." If he doesn't sit, do nothing. Do not give a treat or say a word. Let him figure out what provides him with a tasty dividend and what doesn't.

You need only invest a few minutes each day in clicker-training sessions with your cat. Felines learn best in mini-sessions, not marathon lectures. Their attention spans tend to evaporate after 5 or 10 minutes. Conduct your training sessions in a quiet place where you can work without distractions. Time the training before a meal, so that your hungry cat will be more motivated to learn.

Using a clicker, you can train your cat to perform a few basic commands as well as other things limited only by your imagination and your cat's preferences. You can teach your cat to do the cha-cha, for example, if he likes to walk forward and backward when he follows you into the kitchen. You can also train your cat to move in a circle, shake with his front paw, or even meow on cue.

The beauty of clicker training comes in the payoff. You end up with a more mentally stimulated cat and a stronger friendship bond with him. Once your cat is consistently completing some clicker-trained tricks, stage a performance for your husband and watch his amazement at these feline feats. 🐾

Top 10 Rules for Training Cats

Whether you elect to use a clicker or simply voice commands or hand gestures, here are some pointers that will make training easy and fun for you and your cat.

- Always say your cat's name to get his attention before giving any command.

- Be consistent with your verbal and hand signals.

- Pay attention to your cat's mood. Train him when he is receptive to learning, not when the lessons fit your schedule.

- Select a quiet time and room where you can be one-on-one with your cat.

- Be positive, patient, and encouraging.

- Provide small food rewards and enthusiastic praise immediately after each success, no matter how small.

- Start with the basic commands of *Come*, *Sit*, and *Stay*.

- Break the desired behavior into smaller steps and build on each one.

- Teach your cat only one new trick or behavior at a time. Cats are not multitasking masters.

- Keep training sessions simple and short—no more than 5 to 10 minutes at a time.

CATS ARE GAME FOR GAMES

My workload has picked up and it seems like I have limited spare time. And I think it is affecting my young cat, Milton. Lately, he dashes into the bathroom and shreds the toilet paper into confetti. He leaps on my coffee table to send my magazines flying across the living room floor. Any ideas on what I can do?

Your suspicions are correct. Milton is desperately trying to get your attention and to battle boredom. With no structured interactive play activities, home-alone cats are forced to seek less-than-desired options to pass the time. They may nap too much or eat too much or, worse, engage in destructive behavior in frustrated attempts to banish boredom and loneliness.

It doesn't have to be that way. Cats need and deserve purposeful play. Why not set aside 5 to 10 minutes each day and engage in interactive games with Milton? Trust me, it will be worth every minute to you both.

Here are three of my favorite people-cat games that are fun, inexpensive, and simple.

Kitty in the Middle. To play this game, position Milton between you and a family member or friend in an open area such as a hallway or spacious living room. Crinkle a paper wad or store-bought cat sparkle ball to garner your cat's attention. Toss the object just over your cat's head to the other person. Toss back and forth, allowing your cat to leap up and snap the flying "prey" and heap on the praise when he does.

Feline Fishing. Tap in to your tabby's inner hunter by cutting the handles off a brown grocery sack. Open the bag and cut a small hole in the bottom. Place the bag on its side. Then attach a toy mouse or other small cat toy to the end of a long shoelace. Thread the shoelace through the hole, leaving the toy just at the open top of the bag. Show Milton the toy, then wiggle the shoelace to entice him to pounce. Pull the string so he dives after the mouse into the bag.

feline fact

A cat can jump five to six times his own height.

The Great Kibble Hunt. Go bowl-less once a week. At mealtime, put Milton in an enclosed room and then scatter a portion of kibble in a long hallway or on each stair. Then encourage him to sniff out and track down each piece of food and praise him for his finding skills. You can also bring out his innate hunter and make him work for his food by placing a portion of his daily kibble in a treat ball that requires him to swat it around to make the food fall out.

Provide Milton with toys he can enjoy solo when you are away from home. Tie a thick shoelace around a doorknob and attach a dangling toy mouse for him to swat. When you are home, toss a couple of crinkly cat balls or table tennis balls in the empty bathtub for him.

Finally, keep the bathroom door shut and stash your magazines in a drawer to thwart Milton from his feline mischief. 🐾

BECOMING A FELINE FOSTER PARENT

I worked hard for 40 years and am now retired, but I don't have the travel bug or any desire to play golf. I enjoy doing projects at home and want to be an active volunteer in my community. I love cats, and my friends' cats seem to like me. What does it take to be a feline foster parent for kittens or cats at my local animal shelter?

I am betting that your local shelter would welcome you with open arms and heaps of gratitude. There is always a need for volunteers who possess the special ability to nurture and bring out the healthy best in their sheltered cats and kittens. Shelters need people like you who know that the feline's stay may be temporary until the animal lands a loving forever home.

Shelters carefully screen foster candidates, so expect a background check to make sure you don't have any animal cruelty or human abuse charges. If you rent, they will obtain verification from your landlord that it is okay for you to bring in shelter animals to foster.

Here are some insights to become a successful foster pet parent:

- Pet-proof your home before the shelter feline arrives. (See Cat-Proofing Your House, page 47.)

- Make sure your own pets are current on their vaccines. Often, shelter animals sent to foster homes are very young or recovering from an injury or illness and need added attention. They may have still-developing or weakened immune systems. Work with your veterinarian to ensure your own pets are at their healthy best to minimize risk to them and these furry visitors.

- Provide safe play toys—and remember to play. Forgo strings and/or toy mice that contain small items that could choke a kitten. Opt for feather wands and balls they can stalk and chase.

Schedule regular play sessions each day and you will find yourself feeling happier and healthier, too.

- Serve up healthy chow. Adhere to the foster pet's dietary needs to minimize any chance for gastrointestinal issues.

- Be willing to learn new pet skills. You may get the opportunity to master the art of bottle feeding, for example.

As for the rewards one receives by fostering? Priceless. As a foster parent, you will be giving shelter kittens and cats the best possible chance to land a permanent, loving home. Your job is to care for them and to love them until they are ready for adoption. I'm betting that you will find your retirement years blissfully full and fun thanks to opening your home to felines in need. 🐾

Feline Will Power

Do you have a plan in place in the event your cat outlives you? Educating pet parents about this need is Amy Shever, founder and director of 2nd Chance 4 Pets, a nonprofit, all-volunteer advocacy group that provides information and solutions—including pet trusts—to help pet owners make plans for "lifetime care" for their pets.

The group's goal is to reduce the number of beloved pets relinquished and euthanized each year due to the death or disability of their owners. Regardless of age, every responsible pet owner needs to have a plan of care should their pets outlive them.

She offers these tips for pet owners.

Choose the plan that best fits your situation. Your choices include a pet trust or specifying care instructions for your pet in your will or estate documents.

Choose caregivers now who agree to care for your pet if you die or are not physically able. Carry an emergency pet ID card with you that contains the names and contact numbers for these designated caregivers.

Create a written plan that states exactly how you want your pet to be cared for, including the type of food, grooming, and other activities.

Provide money for your pet's care. And if your pet dies with money left in the fund, predetermine where that money should go—say an individual or a pet charity.

Talk about it. Let trusted friends and family members know where your trust or other document is and let them know your care plans for your surviving pets. Provide a copy of your cat's estate plan to your veterinarian.

A CAT'S AGE IN HUMAN YEARS

Figuring out your feline's age can be a frustrating exercise. The myth of "one cat year equals seven human years" is just that—a myth. Cats reach senior status by the age of 7 and are considered geriatric by the age of 12.

While there is no reliable scientific method for converting your cat's age into human years, experts report that at 1 year of age, a cat is roughly equal to a 15-year-old human. The following chart gives you an idea of your cat's age in people years.

LIFE STAGE	AGE OF CAT	COMPARABLE HUMAN AGE
KITTEN	0–6 months	0–10 years
JUNIOR	7 months–2 years	12–24 years
PRIME	3 years	28 years
	4 years	32 years
	5 years	36 years
	6 years	40 years
MATURE	7 years	44 years
	8 years	48 years
	9 years	52 years
	10 years	56 years
SENIOR	11 years	60 years
	12 years	64 years
	13 years	68 years
	14 years	72 years
GERIATRIC	15 years	76 years
	16 years	80 years
	17 years	84 years
	18 years	88 years
	19 years	92 years
	20 years	96 years
	21 years	100 years

USEFUL WEBSITES

American Association of Feline Practitioners
www.catvets.com

American Society for the Prevention of Cruelty to Animals
www.aspca.org

American Veterinary Medical Association
www.avma.org

ASPCA Animal Poison Control Center
www.aspca.org/apcc

The Cat Fanciers' Association
https://cfa.org

Cat Friendly Homes
https://catfriendly.com

Cat Lovers' Academy
www.catloversacademy.com

Catster
www.catster.com

Cat Writers' Association
www.catwriters.org

Community Cat Podcast
www.communitycatpodcast.com

EveryCat Health Foundation
www.everycat.org

Fear Free Happy Homes
www.fearfreehappyhomes.com

Fear Free
www.fearfreepets.com

Hauspanther
www.hauspanther.com

Indoor Pet Initiative
https://indoorpet.osu.edu

KittyCatGO
https://kittycatgo.com

Lost Cat Finder
www.lostcatfinder.com

Love on a Leash
www.loveonaleash.org

Nextdoor
https://nextdoor.com

Pet First Aid 4U
www.petfirstaid4u.com

Pet Life Radio
www.petliferadio.com

Pet Partners
https://petpartners.org

Pro Pet Hero
www.propethero.com

RECOMMENDED READING

Cat Facts: The Pet Parent's A-to-Z Home Care Encyclopedia by Amy Shojai, Furry Muse Publications, 2017

Catification: Designing a Happy and Stylish Home for Your Cat (and You!) by Jackson Galaxy and Kate Benjamin, TarcherPerigree, 2014

Cat Scene Investigator: Solve Your Cat's Litter Box Mystery by Dusty Rainbolt, Stupid Gravity Press, 2016

CatWise by Pam Johnson-Bennett, Penguin Books, 2016

Decoding Your Cat: The Ultimate Experts Explain Common Cat Behaviors and Reveal How to Prevent or Change Unwanted Ones, by American College of Veterinary Behaviorists, Houghton Mifflin Harcourt, 2020

The Original Cat Bible by Sandy Robins, Fox Chapel Publishing, 2014

Pounce! A How to Speak Cat Training Guide by Gary Weitzman and Tracey West, National Geographic Kids, 2020

ACKNOWLEDGMENTS

I give plenty of grateful purrs to all the animal behaviorists, veterinarians, and professional cat trainers who have guided me for the past two decades of learning all things c-a-t. Special thanks to Dr. Liz Bales, Dr. Marty Becker, Kathy Black, Dr. Debora Charles, Dr. Elizabeth Colleran, Dr. Jean Hofve, Stacy LeBaron, Teresa Keiger, Samantha Martin, Dr. Arnie Plotnick, Dr. Kathryn Primm, Dr. Lisa Radosta, Dusty Rainbolt, and Rita Reimers.

I also give much appreciation to Lisa Hiley, my main editor, and the entire Storey Publishing team, who have believed in me since they published my first pet book more than 20 years ago.

INTERIOR PHOTO CREDITS

INDEX

Love Your Pets
with More Books by Arden Moore

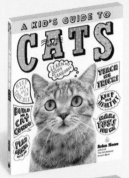

A Kid's Guide to Cats
Learn everything you want to know about your kitty friends, from what makes them tick to how to keep them healthy, with plenty of fun along the way.

A Kid's Guide to Dogs
Learn all about breeds, body language, training, health care, and make-them-yourself dog treats and toys!

The Dog Behavior Answer Book, 2nd Edition
The browsable Q&A format offers practical advice and workable solutions to common problems.

Join the conversation. Share your experience with this book, learn more about Storey Publishing's authors, and read original essays and book excerpts at storey.com. Look for our books wherever quality books are sold or call 800-441-5700.